Among the twenty-five books written by Oscar Schisgall are *Swastika, The Big Store, The Mountains Are My Kingdom, Wings of Wrath,* and *The Man from Nowhere.*

THE MAGIC OF
MERGERS

MESHULAM RIKLIS

THE MAGIC OF MERGERS

The Saga of Meshulam Riklis

by

OSCAR SCHISGALL

LITTLE, BROWN AND COMPANY
BOSTON • TORONTO

Published simultaneously in Canada
by Little, Brown & Company (Canada) Limited

PRINTED IN THE UNITED STATES OF AMERICA

A Foreword for
Curious Millionaires

THIS is an adventure story — adventure in American business during an unprecedented era of multimillion-dollar mergers.

It is also a biography, since it deals with the career of an extraordinary businessman, Meshulam Riklis. If his rise were marked on a chart it would show a climb in a single decade — when he was still in his twenties and thirties — from nothing to the summit of a tremendous industrial complex. Then, abruptly, there would be a precipitous dip. And immediately afterward the line would trace a steep climb to heights loftier than ever.

In gathering material for this study I talked with many industrial leaders who had amassed fortunes of their own. All asked the same question: How had Mr. Riklis done it?

Donald L. Miller, executive vice president of the First National Bank of Boston, said, "To me the most remarkable thing about the man is the fact that hardly four years ago, in 1963, he was considered to be defeated, finished, cast aside by the business community. Yet here he is today, honored, respected; Chairman of the Board of the Rapid-American Corporation, of the McCrory Corporation, of the Glen Alden Corporation, all of which add up to a billion-dollar empire;

vii

the recipient of countless awards and citations. How, in less than four years, did Riklis climb out of the depths and rise to billion-dollar heights? And what kind of character traits does it take to achieve such a success?"

Such puzzled inquiries made me feel that perhaps I was really writing a mystery story.

I hope this book will answer some of the queries that intrigue Mr. Miller and other business leaders. To do so it will be necessary, of course, to study not only Meshulam Riklis's methods but to appraise them against the background of the economic system in which he operates. What is possible in the United States may not always be possible elsewhere; for nowhere is the trend of business mergers so widely prevalent and so efficiently developed as in America.

Riklis's genius, if that is the word for it, lies in being able to make the most of this modern trend. He has some very definite theories — like his insistence on having every industrial acquisition produce enough cash (or its equivalent in borrowing power) to offset its purchase price, thus making additional acquisitions immediately possible.

Another of his basic creeds is one he expresses this way: "No deal is a good deal unless it benefits both parties concerned and unless both are content." Since mergers depend on negotiations among men, this belief is a significant factor in his approach. As a preliminary to any offer he makes to a company, Riklis tries to learn — often by simple, direct questions — what the other man wants. "If I can provide it or help him get it, we have grounds for discussion," he says. "If what he wants is beyond anything I can reasonably offer, there is no point in wasting time in talk." This is a practice to which I shall have to refer frequently in this study; it will explain many actions.

A third facet of his business philosophy is an insistence on healthy reserves of capital. He prefers to borrow rather than to deplete those reserves. Once, in addressing graduate students at the Harvard School of Business Administration, he explained his principle in this manner: "If you know I have a thousand dollars in the bank you won't hesitate to lend me a hundred. But if you know I've already spent my thousand you may have doubts about giving me any money at all."

Finally, in addition to such pragmatic credos, I should mention a characteristic which, while applicable to many American industrial leaders, has become a cardinal tenet for Riklis. This is the acceptance of social responsibility. It reaches into many areas — religious, educational, health, artistic, economic. "He has made his personal business success the cornerstone of a much broader kind of success," said Dr. Bernard Mandlebaum of the Jewish Theological Seminary. "Meeting humanitarian needs is a practice which American private enterprise has adopted with great generosity. Riklis has carried it far beyond the average."

In fact, I was once amused to hear a professional fund raiser observe, "I know how much Rik gave to charity of his own money last year, a tremendous sum, and let me tell you this: that man just doesn't understand the value of a dollar!"

But again, such giving is part of the American tradition. Rik has adopted it faithfully.

In the interests of chronological accuracy I should perhaps begin with the report of an early discussion I had with Riklis. It occurred at the time I decided that he would be the most fitting prototype I could find for any account of how fortunes can be made by means of mergers and acquisitions. Obviously I would need his cooperation to do this. I would require his own interpretation of everything that had happened to him; and I would need the recollections of his family, of his close associates, of many other people.

With this in mind I told him what I intended to do. He looked at me in surprise. We were in his office, talking across his desk, and he asked: "How much do you know about me?"

"Enough," I answered, "to believe you're the kind of man I want for this study."

"Do you realize I'm only forty-two?" he protested. "Nobody writes the biography of a man of forty-two. He hasn't lived long enough to make a life story."

"You've crowded enough into forty-two years," I said, "to prove the point I want to make."

"What point?"

"That the American economy has taken a new tack. That it's now possible, through mergers, to pioneer in new directions."

Riklis picked up a pencil, studied it. "You know," he said after a silence, and with a curious note of humbleness, "this *is* a wonderful country — far more wonderful than I dreamed it would be when I first came here. If your purpose is to show what people can accomplish in America, I'll be glad to go along. I owe the country that. But I'll do it only on one condition — that you talk to others before you question me."

I was not sure of what he meant.

He explained, "It's possible that as you study my life you'll become disillusioned. You may find people who criticize me. You may, somewhere along the line, begin to feel that you picked the wrong man — and you'll regret you ever started with me. That will embarrass us both."

I could not help smiling. From my knowledge, incomplete as it was, I felt confident that he was the ideal exemplar of the merger age.

"What people do you want me to talk to?" I asked.

"Anybody you think of, anybody I've done business with. Talk to those who claim they lost money because of me as well as those who made money. People who bought with me and people who sold me their companies. After you've talked to them all, if you still feel you want to go ahead with this project, I'll give you all the help and information you need. If you decide I'm not your man, we'll just shake hands and forget it. Agreed?"

"You've got a deal," I said.

My preliminary investigations took me to almost every city that had played a part in Riklis's career: Minneapolis, Cincinnati, Chicago, Tulsa, many more. I talked with scores of businessmen. It was in many ways a candid search for somebody who would criticize his methods.

A couple of months of such inquiries confirmed my confidence that I had selected the right man. I remember, for instance, the excitement of Sid Luckman in Chicago — one of two partners who had once sold Riklis their Cellu-Craft company. Luckman — whom Chicago refers to as "Mr. Football" — said with deep vehemence, "This man Riklis is the answer to that old nonsense about 'good guys finish last.' I myself used to think that the only way to win in business is to fight the way you do in a football game — crashing through the line, trampling over the other fellow when necessary. But Rik doesn't crash and he doesn't trample. His story tells how a man can *think* his way to success. It can be an inspiration for any business generation."

Thus he touched upon the very core of what I hoped to demonstrate — that new vistas of success are constantly opening in the United States for people with imagination and initiative.

Another man I saw — William Renchard, Chairman of the Board of the Chemical Bank New York Trust Company — leaned back from his desk, clasped his hands behind his head, and looked at the ceiling.

"You know," he said, "by and large this country has, in my opinion, the most honest people in the world. You may read about crime and crooks and wheeler-dealers who try to swindle the public out of millions. But they are the rare exceptions. The real gauge of American honesty is this: less than one quarter of one per cent of borrowers ever default on bank loans. That's what makes this age of credit possible." Then Mr. Renchard gave me a level look. "For me Rik exemplifies this spirit of the American businessman — this pride in integrity, if you want to call it that. Rik is one man whose signature I don't need on paper. His handshake is all I require."

Two months of such interviews, of delving deep into a man's past, resulted in my returning to Rik's office to resume the conversation we had tabled when first we discussed the project.

"You make the kind of mergers that can be described with dignity," I said. "I'm ready to go ahead."

Riklis smiled and offered his hand across the desk. "In that case we're in business," he said. "I never thought I'd go into a merger with a writer."

Part One

THE YEARS OF PREPARATION

I

IT IS not easy to draw the diagram of a dream. Seventeen years ago, in the living room of his Minneapolis home, a young man of twenty-six tried it. He drew a circle at the top of a sheet of paper while two friends watched in perplexity.

"This," he explained in a pragmatic tone as if he were delivering a lecture, "represents the first company we will buy. The kind of company I have in mind will generate enough cash and enough borrowing power to help us acquire another company."

Below the first circle he drew a second, connected the two with a straight line.

"Now we have two companies working for us. We will use the cash and credit *they* generate to buy a third." He drew a larger circle, joining it to the others. "By making a number of such acquisitions and mergers over a period of, say, ten years we can build an organization worth millions."

His wife, a slim and attractive blond girl who entered the room to serve coffee to the visitors, looked as buoyant and confident as the young man himself. She had long ago learned that though her husband had dreams which might sound extravagant, they generally proved to be practical. She knew he had a way of subjecting plans to mathematical analysis before he spoke of them.

The two visitors, however, exchanged uncomfortable glances. Their host was slight of build, dark haired, not very tall — in truth, he seemed scarcely more than a boy. How do you reply to a boy who seriously assures you that within a decade he will create an industrial empire worth millions? How do you reconcile such possibilities, or impossibilities, with the fact that as he sits there drawing circles he has less than $500 in the world?

Moreover, he had been in the United States only four years — three of them as a college student — so that he was a complete stranger to the American world of finance. And yet he was talking easily, with his unmistakable foreign accent, of companies he intended to merge into a huge financial entity.

True, he now had a job with a Minneapolis stockbrokerage firm, Piper, Jaffray, and Hopwood. Mr. Palmer Jaffray had recently hired him on the strength of recommendations from three professors at Ohio State University. But his job, though it bore the fairly dignified title of junior analyst, was hardly more than that of a trainee. It kept him in a back room, poring over the annual reports, balance sheets, and proxy statements of countless corporations, large and small.

His two friends could not be blamed for their embarrassed silence. Finally one of them, an advertising executive named Robert Miller, pointed at the paper. "Let's go back to that first circle," he said. "You say that as a starter you plan to buy a small company."

"Right."

"With what?"

"With the backing of a syndicate of investors," the young analyst replied. "There are a good many people with money in Minneapolis. If I show them a company with excellent poten-

4

tials, one that can be bought at an attractive price, some of them will come along."

"In other words, you plan to do all this with other people's money?"

The junior analyst could have argued that the entire American economy is based on using "other people's money." Every corporation that sells its securities, as well as banks, insurance companies, even the government itself — all operate on "other people's money." This has become the American way of life, and it is unrealistic to blind oneself to the fact. The old homilies of thrift, of "buy only when you have enough money saved to pay for what you want," the strong nineteenth-century abhorrence of debt all seem to have disappeared. We have arrived at an age which substitutes credit for cash. We compute a person's current buying power in terms of his future earning power, not by what he has in the bank. We apply the same standards to corporations. And America's unprecedented prosperity may be regarded as justification for the change.

Robert Miller could have no objection to forming an investment syndicate. He was familiar with several of them. But in all the others the leaders were invariably men of substance who had a share in the syndicate's investment. This young analyst had nothing of his own to contribute except enthusiasm.

Now the other visitor, a teacher named Haim Bernstein, asked with a trace of irony, "Just when do you plan to launch this multimillion-dollar enterprise?"

"First I've got to find a company I want to buy," the analyst said. "I'm studying various possibilities. Then I've got to organize the syndicate. But it won't be long now."

5

That was in the autumn of 1951. If Haim Bernstein and Robert Miller thought their friend's dreams were grandiose and irrational, who could blame them? Only an immature mind, not yet hardened by life's realities, could seriously discuss such plans. At any rate, so it seemed that day in 1951.

Fifteen years later, in the summer of 1966, I sat with the same dreamer, Meshulam Riklis, on the terrace of his waterfront home near New York. He was not quite forty-three now, but there were touches of gray in his hair. He was somewhat heavier than he had been, of course, but still trim, brisk, and confident.

I had followed him outdoors reluctantly, for it had been fascinating, inside the house, to study the scores of plaques and citations he had received for his participation in charitable causes. Clearly he had learned how to assume the obligations of a man who now directed a $1,300,000,000 industrial empire.

In recent years *Fortune* magazine had twice published long articles discussing his financial career. The fluctuation of his reputation with that publication's editors can be judged by the titles of the stories. In February of 1962 it was a laudatory "The Man Who Made the McCrory Corporation." Eighteen months later it was a harsh "Who's to Blame for Riklis?" (By 1965, however, he was once more being listed in the magazine's roster of financial leaders.)

Other publications too, newspapers as well as periodicals like *Barron's, Forbes,* and *Business Week,* had devoted long columns to his activities. There were outbursts of admiration from writers who called him "brilliant," "a financial genius," and there were sardonic and castigating pieces by others. The most bitter critics were those who were convinced that nobody could *honestly* build an empire with annual sales of $1,300,-000,000 as quickly as Meshulam Riklis had done it.

Once, when I questioned one of these critical writers, he confessed, "To me Riklis is an enigma. I don't understand the methods he has pursued; and frankly, what I don't understand I mistrust." This struck me as a rather frail foundation for an opinion. Yet investigation among other critics emphasized the point that many of them regard Riklis as a man of mystery; and men of mystery always disturb those who are mystified.

Curiously enough, there is very little mystery about the man. With those who approach him frankly he is always outspoken — and usually amused by their perplexed queries.

On that summer afternoon, seated on his terrace, we faced the glitter of Long Island Sound. We could have enjoyed the vistas of blue water and sailboats and the distant Connecticut shore. But instead we concentrated on a sheet of yellow paper that lay on the glass table between us.

At its top Meshulam Riklis drew a small circle exactly as he had once done in Minneapolis. But this time it no longer represented a plan. It symbolized an actuality.

"This is our parent company, the Rapid-American Corporation," he said. "We formed it in 1957 by merging Rapid Electrotype and American Colortype. With the cash and borrowing power this first merger generated we were able to make additional acquisitions. In time we acquired" — he drew a larger circle, connecting the two — "51 per cent of the McCrory Corporation, as well as the McLellan and Green variety stores. McCrory, you might say, became our mainstay. Through it we bought the Oklahoma Tire and Auto Supply stores, the Lerner Shops, the Klein department stores."

Now he drew a much wider circle.

7

"And eventually we were able to buy the Glen Alden Corporation. Glen Alden itself already owned textile plants, the RKO theaters, Blue Coal, and other subsidiaries, all of which became part of our complex. Then recently we acquired a substantial interest in the Philip Carey Corporation, which manufactures building materials." He symbolized this with still another circle. "We also bought the Joseph H. Cohen Company, the country's largest manufacturer of men's clothing; and McCrory acquired the Best department stores; and just lately Glen Alden merged with the BVD Corporation, which is itself a consolidation of twenty companies."

At this point Meshulam Riklis looked up from the yellow paper.

"You understand," he said, "that this diagram does not include the many other interests we bought and sold over the years. There were the Butler stores, the Smith-Corona Typewriter Company, National Shirt Shops, citrus groves, a plastic bag company, and quite a few more. At times we disposed of holdings which were unprofitable. At other times we sold some in order to raise cash for what we considered more attractive opportunities. This chart cannot show all such details."

Nor, I realized, did the circles reveal the problems, the difficulties, the disappointments and failures that had been part of creating an enormous industrial empire. They could not tell of the long periods of negotiations — anywhere from six months to a year and a half — that preceded every merger. They said nothing of the scores of people involved in every deal: not only the principals themselves but their lawyers, their accountants, their chief executives, their bankers, and the representatives of every other group concerned. They did not describe the endless meetings and bargainings, the disagreements and compromises, that marked every conference. What these circles did represent was only ultimate success.

I could not help asking, "Where will it all lead? How many more circles will there be?"

"There are several major acquisitions for which we are now planning," Riklis said. "If they succeed they should put our annual sales well above $2,000,000,000. Beyond that — who can say?"

"You mean there's no limit to this kind of growth?"

"Why should there be a limit? Don't most of us always want to push on to something bigger, something more challenging? I'm sure that after we've put men on the moon we'll want to put them on Mars. Always to push on is the great adventure of life. Maybe it's the only way we can justify the few years we spend on earth."

"But who *benefits* from such growth?"

"Everybody. Take our employees — about 65,000 of them now. We can provide them with pension plans, scholarship funds, and other benefits it would be impossible to manage if we were a small company. As for our stockholders, they gain potential earning power every time we make another acquisition. And it goes without saying that when we buy in enormous quantities for over 1,500 retail outlets we can afford to give consumers the benefit of such mass purchasing power. So I say everybody benefits."

Finally I asked if there was any chance of the government's contending that his empire was becoming *too* big.

"Among all the merchandising companies in the United States," Riklis answered, "there are still twenty-nine larger than we are. We're catching up, but so far we don't have to worry about our size — not as long as there is a General

Motors with $22,000,000,000 in sales or an A. T. & T. with $33,000,000,000."

I remembered then something this man's father had once said to me with quiet pride: "My son was always good at mathematics. Even as a boy he never had trouble calculating in the billions."

2

Whether this era of business mergers has helped to make men like Meshulam Riklis or whether men like Riklis have made this era no one can say. The important thing is that a number of American financiers have to a remarkable degree developed the art of creating vast wealth by combining existing organizations.

In a single year, 1965, more than 2,000 major mergers were consummated throughout the United States. By major mergers I mean transactions measurable in millions of dollars. In the first six months of 1966 there were approximately 1,200 more. Thereafter the trend continued at an even faster pace.

What is causing the phenomenon? The obvious explanation is that the masters of merger tactics are demonstrating a quick, effective, and brilliant way of amassing fortunes. They succeed; therefore they have thousands of would-be imitators. Many a man, I suspect, is secretly the victim of a gnawing frustration which says, "If men like Meshulam Riklis can do it, if men like Norton Simon and Charles Bluhdorn and Nathan Cummings and Charles Thornton can do it, why can't I?"

One is tempted to reply, "Why can't we all run a 3:57 mile? Why can't we all paint a Mona Lisa?"

There are today about twenty men in the United States who are regarded as the giants of empire building. For the purposes of this book I could have analyzed the career of any one of them. If I chose Meshulam Riklis as the prototype, it is because — paradoxical as it may sound — he is at once the most typical and the most extraordinary.

For one thing, he is a purist in the business. The incredible billion-dollar empire he has built grew completely out of acquisitions and mergers. Most other men began by earning their original fortunes in some basic enterprises. Henry Ford had his own great industry before he reached out for the Philco Corporation. Sol Kittay of BVD was called the king of men's underwear before he began assembling companies in other lines. Charles Bassine of Spartans Industries had his apparel factories. The heads of the Textron Corporation had developed an immense textile business before they began to seek firms in the automotive, optical, metal-working, and power-tool fields. The same can be said of the people at General Dynamics, at Olin Mathiesen, at Minnesota Mining and Manufacturing, at hundreds of other corporations.

But Riklis never had a factory, a business, or a profession. In other words, before he began making acquisitions he had no profitable base of operations whatever, no safe haven to which he could retreat. All he had was a $50-a-week job with Piper, Jaffray, and Hopwood. Starting with that, he followed the single course of acquiring and merging existing facilities. He owes his financial position to no other enterprise. That is why I call him a purist.

Moreover — and this is not said to be chauvinistic — his career attests eloquently to the opportunities still available in the United States. It mocks all those head-shaking economists who used to maintain that with high taxes and the overwhelming competition of industrial giants few individuals could ever again achieve the kind of millionaire status men had earned in the past.

Riklis confounds such solons. Coming to this country twenty years ago with his young wife and daughter, he was a boy who knew practically nobody, who had no funds except enough savings to see him through a year of college, whose background lay in the struggling little area that was still called Palestine.

And yet, in less than twenty years, this man — who became an American citizen fifteen years ago — has risen to head one of the great industrial complexes of the United States; one which he assembled by his own efforts.

Few businessmen have stories to match the Riklis record for color and excitement in the area of mergers. In truth, when one speaks of mergers today one cannot ignore the Riklis saga; and when one speaks of the Riklis saga, one cannot ignore mergers. The two are inseparable.

3

It is inevitable that legends and anecdotes should gather around a man whose interests have been so widespread and dramatic. I have heard most of these stories, and some I have discarded; but one cannot discard the testimony of eyewitnesses who speak from their own experience.

For instance, one of Riklis's oldest associates, Melvin Unterman who used to be a Minneapolis manufacturer of outerwear, recalls the time six years ago when he sat in Chicago's Pump Room with Rik and a Los Angeles investment banker, B. Gerald Cantor of Cantor, Fitzgerald and Company. "Some weeks earlier," Mr. Unterman says, "we had discussed my interest in a Chicago bank. I had looked for an appropriate bank, one whose stock might be acquired without too much trouble, and I had located the ideal situation. At this Pump Room luncheon I talked it over with Rik and Cantor.

"When I finished, Riklis asked the waiter for a telephone. As we continued talking and eating lunch he made half a dozen calls from our table. He spoke to men in Minneapolis, in Cincinnati, in New York; men who had previously joined him in other ventures and who had made money through him. He put the proposition so simply that I thought he'd be laughed at. All he said was, 'Mel's going to buy stock in this Chicago bank. It's a good deal. I think you ought to get in on it.'

"It is a measure of the confidence he had won when I tell you that before we left our table Rik had been pledged all the money needed."

Another story which sped around the financial community sounded like an exaggeration when first I heard it. It concerned Riklis's acquisition of the Joseph H. Cohen and Sons clothing company. Wilfred P. Cohen himself, who with his brother had sold the business, had been my friend for many years, and he finally gave me the facts.

"Prior to the Riklis deal twenty-six firms had tried to buy us out," he said. "Every time we set a price they countered with a lower figure. We had been asking $18,000,000 and we repeatedly told brokers we would listen to nothing less. Yet they kept coming back to us with offers of $14,000,000 and $15,000,000. This so annoyed us that we no longer wanted to discuss the matter with anybody. We were tired of bargaining. We gave up the idea of selling.

"At this point one of my associates told me to expect a call from Meshulam Riklis.

"I had heard of Riklis but I had never had a chance to know

13

him. I felt sure he was another of those wheeler-dealers who would try to argue me into coming down in price. When he telephoned that afternoon I thought, 'What's the use of getting into a hassle? I'll give him a price that will shut out all conversation, and that will be that.' So when Riklis told me he'd like to see me about buying Joseph H. Cohen and Sons, I said, 'There's no use talking unless you're ready to pay our price.'

"Rik asked, 'What *is* your price?'

"To end the farce I threw out a reckless, 'Twenty-one million. Cash.'

"Without hesitation he answered, 'You've got it.'

"I sat stunned. I had expected him to laugh or say something scornful. Instead, without any change of tone, he had accepted my terms. And that's the way the deal was made.

"Don't get the idea that he was being quixotic. I'm sure he had calculated in advance how high he was prepared to go for a company showing profits of over $4,000,000 a year. The fact that he did not argue indicated only that my figure fell within the limits of his calculations. Rik's philosophy includes the belief that if a property is worth buying you don't bargain. You either agree that it's worth the asking price or else you say, 'No, thank you,' and walk away. He never wastes time in arguing."

For myself, one of the most significant traits I have found in Meshulam Riklis is his respect for learning — or, to put it in its simplest terms, for the importance of a college degree. This, I believe, is a feeling his scholarly father implanted in him.

One afternoon in the spring of 1966 I came into his office to find him talking by telephone to the dean of his alma mater, Ohio State University. He was making arrangements to take a summer course which would lead to a Master of Arts degree.

I could not help staring. "At this stage of the game," I asked, "why on earth do you need an M.A. degree?"

"If you have to ask you won't understand," he said.

Throughout the summer Rik flew to Columbus, Ohio, twice a week. He sat in classes with young graduate students, listening to professorial lectures on business and taking notes. Evenings and weekends he worked on his thesis. He called it "Expansion Through Financial Management" and he allowed me to see parts of it as he progressed. The professor with whom he worked must have suggested many changes, all of which Rik made without protest. He rewrote the eighty-page document four times.

"If you knew how much his evenings and weekends mean to him," his long-time secretary, Mary Friedwald, told me, "you'd realize how much he must prize this M.A. degree."

At the end of the summer his wife went to Columbus with him to see him receive the coveted degree. "I have never seen Rik happier," she confided later.

His friend Albert List of the Glen Alden Corporation (now part of the Riklis empire, of course) welcomed him back to New York with a tremendous surprise party. The gathering was attended by bankers, financiers, and industry leaders who had flown to New York from a dozen states in order to salute Rik on the occasion of becoming a Master of Arts. All of them donned cap and gown and stood in line to congratulate him.

Two of his professors had come, too, and I talked with them. "How much would you say Rik learned that he didn't know before he took this summer course?" I asked.

One of the professors smiled. "I can't tell you how much *he* learned," he said. "But the other students got him into long bull sessions after every class, and I can tell you *they* learned plenty! And if you want the full truth, so did the faculty."

Months later it occurred to me that Rik had never hung his new diploma where it could be seen. "You worked hard for that degree," I said. "Don't you want people to know you have it?"

He seemed surprised. "Why should they?" he asked. "I didn't want an M.A. in order to impress anybody. I wanted it just to satisfy myself."

II

To ANALYZE the Riklis operation one must first understand the background, the ambitions, and the circumstances which impelled this man to follow the course he chose.

There are some explanatory generalizations which I have repeatedly heard. Though I do not wholly agree with them, they have been offered by such earnest and thoughtful men that they deserve consideration.

For example, a distinguished banker who happens to be a Methodist once said to me: "You've got to remember that for centuries Jews have had to be imaginative, clever, bold, and aggressive if only to survive. Even before the Nazi era many of them lived at a terrible disadvantage in their ghettos. If they avoided extinction in spite of pogroms, Inquisitions, and Hitlers, it was because of two great qualities: first, an unshakable faith in their God and in the Jewish way of life; and second, remarkable brain-power — the kind of brain-power that could outwit all enemies.

"Even in Israel," this banker continued, "they remained a harassed minority of two and a half million surrounded by the threat of forty million Arabs. There could never be any relaxation of alertness, of the need to outthink adversaries. Riklis is the product of these people — long generations of them. He inherits ethnic traits and mental abilities that go far toward explaining his drive and his success."

Like all generalizations, this may contain *some* element of truth. But being the descendant of countless generations of Jews is certainly not the reason Meshulam Riklis, of all men, was able to build an industrial empire. What the banker said about him can obviously be said about all Jews in Israel. Riklis, however, is the only one who became Board Chairman of the Rapid-American Corporation. Attributing this to ethnic or religious causes is like saying John D. Rockefeller became a millionaire because he was an American Baptist.

To understand Meshulam Riklis and his activities we must appraise the man for himself and for those of his characteristics that are unique. This is not to *discount* the banker's generalized approach. It is only to place it in perspective — that is to say, to make it the backdrop of the stage on which Riklis has been playing his part.

He has had a colorful life; this cannot be denied. His parents were in Istanbul, where Rik's father represented a Palestinian firm, and they decided they would like to have their son born in their homeland, Palestine. Perhaps they should not have tarried as long as they did, or perhaps Rik — in a hurry even before birth — came before his calculated time. At any rate, he was born in Turkey.

The family took him to Palestine as soon as he could travel, and there he was reared. His father, an official of a citrus company, was moderately well-to-do. Like so many Palestinian Jews, he was devoted to learning and to cultural pursuits. For that matter, so was the entire Riklis clan. One of them who followed a musical career, a cousin of Meshulam, is today the conductor of a symphony orchestra. Others turned to the study of law, medicine, the Talmud. There are teachers among them and journalists — representatives of every career that requires education.

Rik's youthful scholastic years took him through Herzlia High School — the excellent school which has been the cradle of so many of Israel's leaders. His father had attended the same institution twenty-five years earlier. (It was recently moved to make room for Tel Aviv's first skyscraper, a thirty-story structure that juts up from the center of the city.)

At Herzlia he was a good all-round student, but his particular forte lay in mathematics. In fact, he astounded the faculty by developing his own formula for Pythagorean numbers — a theory of mathematical progression. His arithmetical understanding was so keen, so quick, so accurate, that he enriched his student days by tutoring less proficient schoolmates. (This ability to deal with figures, to subject them to swift analysis, has been one of his mainstays in the American business world. His present associates in New York echo what has so often been said by Rik's early colleagues in Minneapolis: "He can read more in a balance sheet than any man I ever knew.")

It was during his high school days, when he was fourteen, that he met Judith Stern, a fellow student. Perhaps it would be naive to say that he fell in love at the age of fourteen (though who doesn't?). At any rate, he and Judy paired off in a relationship that continued not only through the school years but into a postgraduate period when both of them joined a *kibbutz*.

Going into a *kibbutz* was, of course, the idealistic way of life for young Palestinians — something like going into the Peace Corps for young Americans today. As it turned out, the agricultural life of the *kibbutz* was not to Rik's taste. It left him restless, dissatisfied. "I guess I'm not emotionally suited to picking bananas and vegetables," he said. At the end of a year he resigned from the settlement.

He was eighteen then. Where the future might have led him he was never to know — for the Near East was embroiled in World War II. The British Eighth Army desperately needed men. War fever inflamed everyone. And Rik enlisted.

When he applied for officers' training he was rejected almost with scorn. He was far too young, he was told. "Why, you've got your mother's milk still on your lips!" He argued that the military tutors of his high school days had ranked him as the number one graduate of the student army corps. Apparently the British Eighth Army thought this might be a fine recommendation if the war were being waged against German high school students. But in the adult fight against Hitler and Rommel — "Sorry, Riklis. No O.T.C."

He became a clerk.

This was the most boring job he had ever undertaken — even worse than the 5 A.M. to 5 P.M. chores in the *kibbutz.*

Why he of all people was eventually assigned to be a chaplain's chauffeur, he never learned. Nevertheless he welcomed the change. At least there would be *action.*

True, instead of crouching heroically behind a machine gun he sat behind a jeep's steering wheel. But he traveled. He saw North Africa. He heard the blast of guns. He knelt over the wounded and helped bury the dead. The chaplain, a rabbi, wanted always to be where he might be most needed — which is to say where the fighting and the casualties were heaviest. So Rik drove Chaplain Auerbach as far as Tunis in the wake of Rommel's forces.

Egypt, Tunis, Italy — wherever the British Eighth Army

went to do its fighting, Rik went too. He spent five years in the thick of warfare yet never operated anything more lethal than the jeep. Sometimes he was so close to enemy lines that he had to cover the car with mud; in that way he avoided having its metallic glints attract Nazi fire.

Those years were no doubt the most important formative period of his life. Spending almost all his days and nights driving beside the chaplains — first Chaplain Auerbach, then Chaplain Berman, both devout, soft-spoken, earnest men — Rik developed a profound respect for rabbinical learning and philosophy. He discovered how exciting it was to *care* about the needs of other men; to analyze their problems; to compare the happy ones with those who were frustrated.

"And in those days I had plenty of time to think," he once told me. "Driving across the desert at night, the rabbi and I might talk now and then — especially when I asked a question — but in between talking I could give my mind the widest kind of latitude."

He began to ask himself what he most wanted of life. The first thing was quite uncomplicated. He wanted to marry Judy. As soon as he could arrange for a leave, he used the opportunity to rush back to Tel Aviv. He and Judy were married when the war was at its most furious stage.

Now that he was a husband at twenty-one, Rik's thoughts had to take on new dimensions. Once this war ended he would have to support Judy as well as himself. The question was — how?

He had no profession, no vocation. The challenge of the future seemed all the more grim when he succumbed to yellow jaundice. This was in North Africa. He spent a miserable month in a military hospital, the only active part of him being his mind. Lying on an army cot, staring at the ceiling, with sweat dripping off his body, he had more time than ever to think.

If there was one thing a man could learn from a boyhood in Palestine, a poor and almost destitute country when compared to some others, it was the importance of wealth. With money you could build; you could exert influence; you had power. Without it you had to seek the help and patronage of those who *did* have money.

Not that wealth for its own sake seemed important. What was important was being able to secure those benefits which accrued through the *control* of money. The one profound conclusion Rik reached was that, to achieve success in life, he had to find a way of owning or controlling significant sums.

The future, as he saw it, would belong to the industrialists, the financiers, and yes, the scientists — the men who could bring new developments to the world. To become one of them, a leader among them, one had first to learn how to control the vast funds they needed. He had a number of leaves during which he discussed all this with Judy.

At the end of the war Rik told her that he wanted to resume civilian life by taking a college course in finance. He needed this as seriously as a fledgling doctor needs hospital training. But the colleges of the Near East did not offer business courses. Everything Rik had learned from his Eighth Army companions told him to seek his education in London.

Judy instantly agreed. There was only one obstacle to leaving for London now: she was expecting a baby. She suggested that they wait until after its birth.

So Rik took a clerk's job with an export firm. He was assigned to handling correspondence. The bewildering problem of writing a good business letter emphasized for him how little he knew about business. "At noon every day I would hurry over to my father's office, and he would help me compose the letters in acceptable business language."

After the birth of the baby — a girl for whom Judy promptly chose the name Simona in honor of her father, Simon Stern — Rik found that his recent earnings as a clerk plus everything he and Judy had saved amounted to $3,000 — surely enough to defray the first year's cost of a college course. As for the other three years, he was confident he would find a means of earning money while he studied. He was ready for London.

But suddenly Judy demurred.

Her friends had warned her that the London winters could be miserable for a baby: cold, foggy, wet, unhealthy. If Rik had to go somewhere to study, why couldn't it be some part of the world that had a warm, healthy climate like Palestine's? Surely there were colleges in other regions which could offer a good financial education.

Rik listened thoughtfully. When he looked at the baby he felt Judy was right. Why subject the child to the chills of the English countryside when he could pick a more attractive area?

In seeking information about colleges he had learned much about American schools. Ohio State University offered a good financial course, and so did the University of New Mexico. The latter had the advantage of a climate somewhat akin to Palestine's.

So Rik abruptly changed his plans. What might have happened to him if he had gone to London, no one can guess. Would he have done in England what he later did in the

United States? Possibly. But the British economy, the British philosophy of trade might have hampered him.

As it was, Meshulam Riklis took his wife and infant daughter to America, where he began a new life on the campus of the University of New Mexico.

Knowing nobody, he called on the rabbi of the community. "I hoped he would introduce Judy and me to a few people, and he did. One was a very wealthy man, a financier named Lionel Rosenbaum. When the rabbi phoned him, Mr. Rosenbaum — whose son Jay turned out to be one of my classmates — asked me to meet him the next day at his stockbroker's office."

Rik kept the appointment. Waiting for Mr. Rosenbaum, he watched the stockbroker's display board in fascination. He had never before seen this American system of recording stock transactions.

Mr. Rosenbaum, a man in his late forties, was genial, friendly, amused by Rik's perplexity concerning the board. "I explained its meaning to him," Rosenbaum told me years later. "You could see astonishment and excitement start in the boy's eyes. He said, 'So I can sit here in New Mexico and make money by buying and selling stocks in New York?' I assured him it was possible. Rik studied the board in absolute silence. Then he turned to me with a broad grin and said, 'That's for me!' "

But he was still a long way from giving serious attention to the purchase of securities. First he had to complete his college work.

The climate in New Mexico was perfect, but within a few months Rik felt he was not getting the kind of specialized education he had hoped to find. From all he could gather from other students and the faculty, the financial course he sought was the one being offered by Ohio State University.

So, after his freshman year, Rik moved his little family to Columbus, Ohio, and enrolled at Ohio State.

He faced an immediate need of money. The $3,000 he had brought to America was almost gone. Now he had to earn enough to support his wife and daughter while paying for his education.

"I found," he said, "that the one commodity I had to offer the people of Columbus was a knowledge of Hebrew. When I took a job as a Hebrew teacher after college hours, I was simply using the language with which I had been brought up. And that was how I earned enough to see us through those three college years."

Judy too wanted a college education. But what could she do about her infant daughter while she went to class? There wasn't enough money to hire a maid. So Judy remained with the baby while Rik attended classes; and he baby-sat while she went to school.

The problem was alleviated later when Rik's mother flew nine thousand miles from Tel Aviv to be with her grand-daughter. Now both Rik and Judy could give Hebrew lessons and attend college. The opportunities promised by America had never looked brighter.

2

As a class assignment at Ohio State University, Riklis was once instructed by Dr. Gilbert Riddle to find a company "that has more cash than the value of its stock in the market."

As Rik interpreted this, the corporation should have more money in the bank, or due from billings, than it would realize if its outstanding securities were converted to cash. This seemed an illogical situation to the young student. How could a corporation's market value be less than its cash assets, provided the company had no overwhelming indebtedness?

Puzzled, Riklis consulted a Columbus stockbroker. He learned that there were many such situations. In fact, one industry, cement, had scores of firms that met Dr. Riddle's specifications. Yet no one Riklis interviewed could adequately explain the reasons.

Obviously, then, the kind of company a sensible man ought to buy was one which returned more cash than its purchase price!

This, it was clear, made it possible to buy a firm *with its own money*, so to speak. How else could you describe a deal that promptly brought control of as much cash as one put into it?

It may well be that Dr. Riddle's assignment has served as a permanent guide for Meshulam Riklis's activities. In later years among the primary questions he always asked concerning a suggested acquisition or merger was this: *How much cash will the deal immediately generate, and will there be enough to make further acquisitions feasible?*

Before his college years little had been written about the skills needed to complete successful mergers; or about the tribulations that would be encountered. A generation or two earlier, in the muckraking era, a number of books and newspapers had lashed out at the evils of those mergers known as trusts. The very word assumed an ugly connotation. ("Trusts" originally signified no more than the concept of stockholders of several corporations putting their interests into the hands of a single centralized Board of Trustees.)

The attacks on trusts were often justified; too frequently these concentrations of wealth gave enormous power to men who misused it. Their abuses were responsible for the enactment of the Sherman Antitrust Act, the Clayton Act, and other legislation aimed at protecting the nation from the venality of "robber barons." Long before Riklis came to America, history dealt copiously with all this as most historians described only the evils of mergers.

As a result few writers discussed the *benefits* of welding separate companies into efficient, profitable, and harmonious entities. Few stressed the *healthy* results that might accrue from intelligent merging. Whatever men like Riklis learned about the process usually had to be self-taught.

In his case a good part of self-education came, in his student days, out of simple, commonsense thinking. Never forgetting that there were corporations whose cash assets exceeded the market value of their stock, he asked himself this question: *Why* should any firm with a healthy cash position, a good reputation, a fine record of earnings, be sold? What inducements could possibly persuade its owners to part with what they had so solidly built? In short, how could *Rik* acquire such a firm?

He spent a great deal of time speculating on this. Eventually several things that might impel a person to sell a good business became clear.

First, there was the obvious case of the man who was becoming too old or too tired to carry on with his accustomed energy. If he had no one to succeed him — no son or near relative — he might very well listen to a generous offer for his holdings.

Second, there were many companies whose management

27

had already (as Rik put it) "passed into the hands of second generations incapable or unwilling to face new challenges." These young people might be glad enough to sell a controlling interest in the firm they had inherited. Some might even welcome a chance to get *out* of the business with a substantial sum of money.

Third, in this age of high-pressure competition, there were many additions even a successful firm might need which could best be achieved through merging with another company: for instance, the services of skilled technicians, of more experienced management; new products to be marketed, valuable patent rights to be acquired; a diversification of interests, a broader distribution system, and so on. Rik had even heard of businessmen whose lack of *education* left them incapable of dealing with modern demands; they sorely needed the sophisticated help they could get by merging.

Fourth, there must be many companies that would sell part of their stock, even a controlling segment, in order to raise immediate working capital for expansion. And expansion was often an essential part of competing with industrial giants.

Fifth, there were always tax problems a businessman had to confront. If he drew large amounts of cash out of his company, the government would take much of it, perhaps most of it, in income taxes. If he allowed it to accumulate in the corporation's treasury, the Internal Revenue Service — functioning under Code Section 531, which Rik had been obliged to study — might impose severe penalty taxes. And finally, if he died his family could lose much of what he left through high inheritance taxes.

Yes, there were many arguments for selling a business; especially the fact that if a man accepted payment in tax-free stock instead of money he paid no taxes at all until he sold the stock. The law did not regard the acceptance of shares as the equivalent of income.

In brief, Rik could see a number of sensible grounds on which a firm might be approached with an offer for its assets. But as a preliminary to such successful negotiation he realized that one ought to spend days, weeks, even months in studying the *needs* of the people whose business one hoped to acquire. Even in his early days he said, "There's no sense making an offer to someone unless you know what he wants most."

He had no illusions that all acquisitions or mergers must be successful. As a matter of fact, the years have shown that about 40 per cent of all mergers, like a similar percentage of marriages, do *not* fulfill the expectations that prompted them.

Often the reasons for failure lie in the inability of two management groups to function together as a team. Each is accustomed to its own policies and practices; and when they are reluctant to change these methods they find it difficult to develop the proper synergy — as the dictionary defines the word, "the cooperative action of two or more body organs." Sometimes the problems posed by a lack of synergy become so harassing that both companies yearn for a divorce — that is, to be divested of each other's troubles.

A case in point arose when two insurance companies merged. It was thought that this move would benefit both of them. Unhappily the people responsible for the merger overlooked or deliberately ignored a factor that quickly became an obstacle to peaceful coexistence: the two companies had widely different salary scales. A vice-president in Company A earned far more than this counterpart in Company B. This was true all the way down the management line.

What, then, was to occur as a result of the merger? Were the high salaries of Company A to be reduced to meet the lower standards of Company B? If that were attempted, most of the Company A executives would resign. On the other hand, Company B had five times as many employees and officers as Company A. To increase all their salaries would cost the corporation millions of dollars. This could turn the merger into a loss operation.

Executives of both firms — plus cohorts of attorneys and accountants—are still grappling with the issue. Meanwhile the problem serves as an indication of the many things that can sour a merger.

Riklis was destined to encounter such perplexing situations in studying the problems of mergers. But he knew little about them the day he was graduated from Ohio State University as a Bachelor of Arts. His first challenge was to find a way of supporting his family in the postgraduate years, while he began studying for a Master's degree. There was now a second daughter, Marcia, just a few months old. His wife's recent confinement had cost every cent they had been able to save from their earnings as Hebrew teachers. Moreover, they had been forced to borrow $70.

So Meshulam Riklis, B.A., just out of college and $70 in debt, needed a job badly.

3

He had discovered that American industry eagerly recruited graduates in engineering and other technical disciplines; but few companies bothered with those who held only Bachelor of Arts degrees. Though he had excellent letters of recommendation from his professors, he knew it might take weeks to find the kind of job he wanted in a financial institution. He could not afford to take the time.

Through his extracurricular work he had heard of a Hebrew school in Minneapolis which needed teachers. Rik went for an interview and found everything in his favor. Because he had been brought up in Palestine when it was a British mandate, he spoke English as well as he spoke Hebrew. He had a college education. He had a pleasing personality, was rather good-looking with his thick dark hair and humorous eyes, and he appeared to have quiet self-confidence. Moreover, he had had several years of experience as a Hebrew teacher.

Not only was he hired; his wife Judy too was offered a teaching job.

In the course of this first Minneapolis interview Rik met a young man of his own age who was to become a lifelong friend. Haim Bernstein also was a teacher at the school. Both had been reared in Palestine — which by this time had become the independent State of Israel. Though Haim Bernstein came from Jerusalem, while Rik had been brought up in Tel Aviv, they found that they had many mutual friends "in the old country."

In a hurry to return to his family in Columbus, Rik asked Bernstein to find an apartment for him. "My wife and I want a place we can move into as soon as we arrive," he said. This would save the expense of living at a hotel. Bernstein accepted the duty and within a few days he sent Rik the address of a flat he had rented.

So, in the summer of 1951, a small rented car towed a rented trailer into the Twin Cities. The car itself contained Rik, his blond young wife, their daughter Mona, and the infant Marcia. The trailer held everything they owned: clothes, a modest assortment of furniture, pots and pans, and the other possessions with which they had lived in Columbus, Ohio.

Their arrival in Minneapolis might have been unobtrusive if it had not been for one sad fact: in the very heart of the city, where traffic was heaviest, the trailer collapsed with a broken wheel.

Rik jumped out of the car in dismay to stare at the wreck. The crowds that gathered were sympathetic, but nobody could replace a wheel. It was a disgruntled traffic policeman who finally sent for a repair truck.

By the time the Riklis family could roll again they were exhausted. Their spirits were bleak. Somewhere on the other side of town was the apartment Haim Bernstein had rented for them, and they drove to it in silence.

When Judy walked into the empty place she could not believe what she saw. Holding Mona by the hand and the baby in her arm, she went slowly from room to room. She stared at a bathtub whose porcelain had peeled away, leaving long streaks of rust. She tried faucets that were corroded. She stood dazed before an ancient stove, dirty, battered, then blinked in amazement at the cracked ceiling, at the peeling walls. And everywhere there was a thick layer of dust, dust, dust.

This was too much. Judy Riklis crumpled down on one of the grips Rik had brought in, and there she wept.

(Years later Haim Bernstein confessed that, having had only a day or two to find a place for his friends, he had accepted the guidance of a real estate agent who assured him nothing better was available at the price in all of Minneapolis or St. Paul. Bernstein had seen the apartment hurriedly and in darkness, thus missing its unpleasant details.)

While Judy sobbed, Rik made his own slow rounds of the rooms. The more he saw the grimmer his expression became. In the end he told her to wait with the children; he had to talk to the real estate agent.

He was gone fully two hours. Judy was becoming desperate. When at last he returned he picked up the grips and said, "Let's go. I've found another place."

He had not only found a place; he had the agent's agreement to cancel the first unfortunate choice.

At twilight they arrived at the apartment they were to occupy for the next few months. The neighborhood was pleasant, its trees and lawns providing a quiet suburban atmosphere. The interior, though small, was clean. Moreover, this place had the advantage of being within a few minutes of the school at which Rik and his wife were to teach Hebrew.

They were home. They put down their suitcases and sat upon them, utterly spent.

(Again years later Haim Bernstein, by that time Rik's business associate in New York, told me, "The way he reacted to a bad break that afternoon, immediately going out to find another apartment, is something I've often thought of as symbolic. You might say it indicated how he would always react to bad breaks — pushing them aside at once and finding something better.")

4

Rik's work at the Hebrew school did not begin until 4:30 in the afternoon, when students were finished with their regular school classes. That meant he could handle another job between 9 A.M. and 4 P.M., a circumstance that could fit in smoothly with the office hours of a stockbrokerage firm. And a

stockbrokerage job would take him where he wanted to be —
into the financial world. It was with the idea of holding both
jobs that he applied for work at Piper, Jaffray, and Hopwood.

Mr. Palmer Jaffray, who interviewed him, was a man of
great dignity; a governor of the New York Stock Exchange; an
elder statesman in the financial community of the Twin Cities.
He was deeply impressed by the letters of recommendation
Rik had brought from his professors at Ohio State. "They were
so full of praise," he once told me, "so full of assurances that
this was one of the brightest students the School of Business
Administration had ever graduated, that I felt our office could
not *afford* to let him get away."

Mr. Jaffray asked many questions. At the outset he had
some doubts about hiring a young Israeli with an obvious
foreign accent; this hardly matched the all-American image of
a house like Piper, Jaffray, and Hopwood. But he slowly
reread the letters of recommendation. Then he folded and
returned them to Rik.

"Start with us on Monday," he said. "You will be working as
a junior analyst under Mr. Ken Scully. The salary will be $50 a
week."

III

"IN MY early days with Piper, Jaffray, and Hopwood," Rik has confessed, "I made every silly mistake a neophyte could make. I even confused a quarterly report with an annual report. Yet these errors never shook the patience or the kindness of my immediate boss, Ken Scully. He would call me to his desk, point out the inaccuracies in my reports, and send me back to my work much wiser and humbler. I used to wonder how many years it would take me to learn even half of what a veteran like Scully already knew."

Nevertheless Rik learned fast. After studying hundreds of balance sheets he began to understand where to seek their significant figures. The investment possibilities on which he had to write reports surprised him, as had similar ones during his college years. There were countless securities that were selling for less than the actual value of their companies. All his instincts told him again that the way to make money was to acquire control of such undervalued firms, to develop them to their full potentialities, to bring the price of their stock at least to the point at which it would represent true worth. Most important, however, would be the use of their assets and sound credit to acquire additional properties.

But to make acquisitions would require not only money, a

great deal of it, but the financial support of investors. How could he come to meet investors while he was a junior analyst? The men at Piper, Jaffray, and Hopwood who *knew* rich people — and meanwhile earned substantial sums — were those who sold securities, the customers' men. Rik had to be one of them.

To sell securities, however, he would need a special license; and to obtain a license he would first have to pass Stock Exchange examinations. So, after several intense months as an analyst ("He worked harder and asked more questions than any man in the office," said Palmer Jaffray) Rik received the firm's approval to apply for a license. He passed the examinations without trouble. In time the license arrived, and this lifted him to the next phase of his career — a customers' man.

His ultimate goal, of course, remained what it had been ever since the day he began drawing circles to indicate how an industrial empire could be built. Now, with his new status, there were certain immediate steps he could take toward his objective.

Before all else he had to prove his ability to help potential backers earn money. He had to win their confidence. If what he hoped to accomplish with their aid seemed imaginative and remote, he had to make them see that it was also practical. This could hardly be done by urging them to confine their investments to the safe but conventional purchase of such blue chip securities as A.T. & T. or General Motors. Any investor could acquire these without the guidance of a counselor. Rik knew that, apart from such orthodox purchases, he must lead his customers into new areas which would surprise them by unexpected yields. Once they discovered they could profit by accepting his guidance, they could be molded into a purchasing syndicate. This in turn would make possible the first acquisitions of the future empire.

At twenty-eight, Rik brushed aside the speculation that it might be difficult to persuade mature, successful businessmen to accept the guidance of a boy half their age. Similarly he shrugged off the obstacle of being a virtual unknown in the community — a kind of alien interloper, if you will, who insisted on ignoring the fact that most investors already had their own customers' men.

These were negative thoughts on which he refused to dwell. As he said to Judy one evening, "How can we get anywhere if we let every doubt scare us off?"

As a customers' man he had a peculiar advantage over his colleagues — the circumstance that he was also a Hebrew teacher. This made him something of a curiosity. The Minneapolis Jewish community had never before known such a combination.

Curiosity about Rik probably stemmed in part from an old-world image of Hebrew teachers. Today, in the United States, the Hebrew teacher in a Reform temple's religious school is apt to be a bright young college man who wants to earn extra money; or a professional public school teacher who wants to add to his income. Nobody is surprised when it turns out he is on his way to becoming a lawyer, a businessman, or anything else.

In the old-world view, however — especially among middle-aged and elderly Jews, of whom there were quite a few in Minneapolis — a Hebrew teacher connoted a different image. Some men still remembered the *melamed* who used to make weekly visits to their homes, preparing them for their own *bar mitzvahs*. He was often a vague, ineffectual, somewhat seedy figure who had found no other way of making a living. True, he enjoyed a certain position of dignity; every teacher had to be respected. But he was certainly not expected to be wealthy or even to concern himself with gaining wealth. Not that he had to be as idealistic as a Talmudist or as wise and full of learning as a rabbi. ("If he were that smart he'd *be* a rabbi.") No, he was usually a good, plodding, inoffensive person whose temperament, unhappily, was not quite adapted to commercial competition. The compensation he received for his teaching was rarely generous, but he was too timid, too retiring, and too insecure to rebel. If ever he lost his job, what else could he do?

So here, in the person of young Meshulam Riklis, the conservative Jewish community found an interesting paradox: a Hebrew teacher who was also a lively, well-informed customers' man for a non-Jewish brokerage house.

In addition, he was an Israeli who had for five years been part of the hard-fighting British Eighth Army — a veteran of North Africa, Cassino, and Anzio; a young man who knew, as did his wife, what it had been like to live with Arab neighbors. It was inevitable that Rik and Judy should become subjects of Minneapolis conversation.

So on those occasions when he telephoned the father of one of his pupils for an appointment to discuss investment possibilities, the answer was apt to be a quick yes. People *wanted* to meet and know him.

As a number of Minneapolis businessmen have assured me, once Rik came to their office or home and began to discuss the merits of a security, his youth, his background, all other oddities were quickly forgotten. This young man knew what he was talking about; he never spoke of a company's potentialities without having studied them thoroughly. He was sure of his subject, matter-of-fact, low-pressured. He did not sell; he suggested. He presented the risks of an investment as well as its merits. At this stage he was more interested in making friends than sales.

Of course he did not rely wholly on the parents of his pupils for broadening his circle of contacts. Some of the personal friends he made — men like his fellow teacher Haim Bernstein, advertising executive Robert Miller, lawyer Irving Schermer, garment manufacturer Mel Unterman — all these introduced Rik to their own friends.

Before long he was bringing Piper, Jaffray, and Hopwood customers they had never known before. As one man at the office told me, "He brought in the cream of the Jewish community."

Whether Meshulam Riklis could have done in the summer of 1966, with the stock market sliding downhill, what he did in the summer of 1952, when prices were steadily rising, is debatable. But such a debate is as futile as wondering how a Democrat like Franklin D. Roosevelt might have fared against a Republican like Abraham Lincoln. There are those who insist that the economic climate of Rik's early days favored him; that it is easier to be financially brilliant on a rising market than during a slump. No doubt they are right. But the fact remains that within a year as a customers' man Rik was earning well over $20,000 annually in commissions.

This figure delighted Judy more than it impressed Rik himself. At her insistence they bought a modest house. She wanted him to own property — an important consideration for one who was trying to emphasize his solidity in the commu-

39

nity. (Besides, a property owner generally had an easier path to bank credit.)

Rik remained calm, not deeply affected by the leap of income from $50 to $400 a week. He seemed to see it only as a normal advance toward his goal. After all, this was what he had planned. It was a gauge of the number of substantial customers he was making. There were now a good many well-to-do men in Minneapolis who had earned profits with his help.

He did not make the mistake of rushing them into demonstrating their confidence. Proper timing, he has always maintained, is one of the primary ingredients of any successful undertaking. There is always the right psychological moment to act. Rik waited until 1953 before he decided the time had come to gather some of his satisfied customers into his first syndicate of backers.

For many months he had been studying the potentialities of various undervalued firms. He wanted to begin by acquiring a controlling interest in a "situation" that would pay well and quickly. He was not interested at this point in making money for himself. That could happen later. At the moment he sought only an opportunity to prove that his syndicate could earn good profits.

By 1953 he had located precisely the kind of company it might be wise to buy as the syndicate's first venture. It was the Marion Power Shovel Company of Marion, Ohio.

2

Meshulam Riklis was only twenty-nine when he set out to form this first syndicate. Fortunately the years of successful dealings in Minneapolis had tended to make his customers forget his youth. What concerned them was that he generally knew what he was talking about when he recommended a purchase.

One by one he sat down with his clients. Usually he drew a circle to symbolize the Marion Power Shovel Company. If control of this company could be bought, it could serve ideally as a base for acquiring more circles. *For Marion Power Shovel had more than $2,000,000 in cash in the bank,* and this sum would come with the purchase. The company had for years been showing respectable earnings.

Why, then, was the price of its securities undervalued? The main reason, he believed, lay in the slackening of its managerial enthusiasm. The man who had owned the largest block of its stock, who had for years lent his driving energy to the company, had died. Now his holdings were lodged in an inactive estate.

Having gone to Marion to study the situation and familiarize himself with the company (he was leaving nothing to chance or to the reports of others) Rik was able to assure his clients that the estate's block of securities could be bought at a reasonable price. This would not constitute a controlling interest; but additional shares, he maintained, could be bought on the open market.

The Joseph brothers, Burton and Roger, represented one of the wealthiest families in Minneapolis. Burton managed the family's granaries. Roger was an attorney. Both men were customers of Rik and had repeatedly profited by his advice. Now Burton, after a long conference, was one of the first to agree to enter the syndicate for the purchase of Marion Power Shovel.

Roger, however, had been stricken by polio. He lay helpless

in a hospital. He could hardly be approached with talk about investments.

But thirteen years later, when I saw Roger Joseph in his law office, he told me a moving story. "Some of our people," he said, "used to think Meshulam Riklis was too brash and unpolished, too much interested in money to care about anything else. He once attended a business meeting in a pink shirt; a thing like that so shocked a few of our local puritans that they still talk about it, as if Rik had walked into a conference naked. Well, maybe he *was* to some extent brash. It's true that he never hesitated to pick up the telephone to call anybody he wanted to see, whether it was Minnesota's Senator, Hubert H. Humphrey, or the president of a bank, or anybody else. If that is brashness, he was indeed brash.

"But let me tell you what happened in my case," Roger Joseph said. "I lay helpless in that hospital. Most of my body was paralyzed. The fact that I could still think clearly was a kind of curse. It made me feel that I'd never be able to function again, that my life was over.

"At this lowest point in my life Meshulam Riklis walked into my hospital room. It wasn't just a visit. When he sat down beside the bed he took papers out of a case, told me what they contained, and asked me to draw up an agreement between himself and those who would become members of his syndicate. I looked at him as if he were insane. Finally I asked, 'What kind of nonsense is this? I'm in no condition to do anything.'

"Rik said, 'You're a lawyer. You can think and you can dictate. You've given me business, and I want to give you business. I wouldn't feel right going to any other lawyer. No reason you can't get somebody in to take dictation after you've had a chance to think about this deal. I hope you can have the papers ready for me in about a week. I'll be needing them then.'

"You probably cannot understand," Roger Joseph said, "what that incident meant to me. It changed my thinking, my feelings. Instead of being utterly hopeless I began to hope. If, as Rik had said, my mind was still clear and I was able to dictate my thoughts, maybe I *could* some day resume my law practice. Yes, I drew up those papers. I knew — I've never kidded myself about it — that he came in with business for one reason only: because he guessed how much it could mean to me at that particular moment. It showed me a side of Rik I'd never seen before, never even suspected. It was a side that is sensitive and generous and understanding of other people's needs.

"Was he brash? Was he apt to be uncouth in dress in those early days? I don't know. What's more, I don't care. For me Meshulam Riklis will always be the man who walked into my hospital room when I was ninety per cent dead, in spirit as in body, and saw only the ten per cent of me that could still function."

3

Though the dozen or so men who formed Rik's first syndicate bought some 10,000 shares of Marion Power Shovel, the company never actually became the "first circle" in the Riklis empire. Its future was destroyed by its own success.

For Marion's price kept soaring. Maybe this was due to the influx of new backing as symbolized by the Minneapolis investors; maybe Marion Power Shovel was merely reflecting the general upsurge of the securities market. Whatever the reason, those who had bought 10,000 shares of Marion soon discovered that they could sell and get out with a quick profit of 30 per cent.

That 30 per cent was even more eloquent for them than Rik's long-range dream. His backers took it. They were grateful to him for steering them to a good thing. They clapped him on the shoulder, asked him to find something else as good. But they did not stay with Marion Power Shovel long enough to acquire control of the company.

Rik was acutely disappointed, though nobody except his wife knew how disturbed he felt by the fact that he had not been able to control the actions of the syndicate. In a way, despite the profits Marion had produced, the venture was for him a failure.

But he was ready for another try.

This time he invited his clients' attention to Balcrank, Inc. of Cincinnati. This was a manufacturer of such diverse hard goods as gas-station equipment and metal furniture. Its earnings had always been good. The company owned a considerable amount of real estate (much of which could be sold to generate cash for expansion); and its stock was even more undervalued than Marion's had been. Shares were selling at $11 when their book value was $18.

Rik's studies in Cincinnati, to which he had made several trips, revealed the fact that 30 per cent of the company's securities could be bought immediately from its owners for about $300,000.

His syndicate readily produced the money. The purchase was made. But this time Rik took a step he had never attempted in the case of Marion Power Shovel.

Accompanied by Robert Miller, one of the investors, he

went again to Cincinnati. There he conferred with Balcrank's officers. He argued that the Minneapolis group, owning 30 per cent of the corporation's shares, should now be represented on the board of directors. As a matter of simple arithmetic, a 30-per cent ownership entitled the Minneapolis syndicate to *two* seats on the board.

The Balcrank executives could not deny this. Certainly they had no reason to make a court issue of the request. So Meshulam Riklis, thirty years of age, became a director of Balcrank, Inc. Robert Miller stepped in as his companion on the board. And for the first time Rik gained the experience — as well as the exhilaration — of helping to direct the destiny of an industrial entity.

Almost immediately he tried once more, as he had in the case of Marion Power Shovel, to induce his associates in Minneapolis to acquire enough additional shares to gain full control of Balcrank. It was, he felt, a sound company with an excellent future. But unless he represented the controlling interest he could never persuade his fellow board members, all conservative men, to sell off the company's real estate in order to raise cash for the acquisition of other businesses.

For the second time in two years the Minneapolis investors faced a choice. With the arrival of new backing Balcrank's stock had risen so high that the original $300,000 investment could be doubled by an immediate sale.

As Robert Miller described the situation, it was this: "Should the men in Minneapolis take their profit — a full 100 per cent — by unloading? Or should they invest more and risk a future recession? After all, how high *could* a stock like Balcrank go? If you've got any common sense you sometimes

45

take your profit and run. That's what the Minneapolis group did.

"After they had sold, Rik and I no longer represented anybody on the board but ourselves, and we went off. We had both bought our quota of the syndicate's stock. And like the others, we made a good profit on the investment. But of course, as had happened in the case of Marion Power Shovel, Rik was not happy. You must remember he was not aiming at earning a few thousand dollars. His sights were as they had always been — *on an eventual empire worth millions.*"

So, in spite of having earned a pleasant sum of money in the Balcrank venture, Rik suffered his second rebuff. He had again been sidetracked from making progress toward his main objective. In a way it might have been called a defeat — a defeat administered by his own backers, by their unwillingness to follow his counsel beyond a certain point.

A wise American named Wendell Phillips once said, "What is defeat? Nothing but education, nothing but the first step to something better." I suspect this is the core of the philosophy which has sustained Meshulam Riklis through the occasional disappointments of his business life.

For out of the Balcrank failure he learned this lesson: In the future it would not be enough merely to lead his syndicate to the *control* of a company. He must also find a way of *controlling the syndicate* as well as the corporation. He must, in short, be in a position to push on to the ultimate goal of using a company's assets to expand the syndicate's holdings.

The opportunity to try again, and along far more ambitious lines, came when Rik discovered an amazing possibility. The Gruen Watch Company of Cincinnati, one of the most solid and best advertised watch companies in the country, could be bought at an undervalued price!

For the past year or two its profits had drastically declined. This, Rik saw as he studied the figures, was due largely to the circumstance that Gruen had undertaken too many low-profit government war contracts. Its earnings on watches had been affected by this concentration on other projects. They had, indeed, dropped almost 50 per cent, and the stockholders were understandably dispirited. It should not be too difficult to purchase their holdings, now selling at $14 to $16 a share.

Rik's further investigations convinced him that the company's factory in Switzerland could easily be sold for $5,000,-000 in cash. There were pending offers at this price which Gruen's management had so far declined. Rik saw a bonanza in the situation. If he could raise $5,000,000 out of this transaction the money would at once enable him to acquire other equities. His career as an architect of mergers would be launched.

The immediate question was: how much would be needed to acquire control of Gruen?

He calculated that the huge block of stock held by the Gruen family would have to be increased by about 20,000 other shares (to be bought on the open market) in order to represent a majority interest in the watch company. The price for such purchases should total about $1,500,000.

Though this was much more than Rik had attempted to raise in previous ventures, he had no misgivings. If he could sell 30 *syndicate units* at $50,000 each, he would have all the money he needed. There were now a number of Minneapolis businessmen — those who had made substantial sums through Rik in the past — who could afford such units. There were others who could afford (in "sub-syndicates") to split the cost of a share in, say, five parts of $10,000 each.

Rik decided to offer his backers this opportunity: They could subscribe only half the necessary amount, $750,000 in cash, provided they were willing to authorize borrowing another $750,000.

So, armed with this idea, Meshulam Riklis set out to acquire a venerable and internationally respected corporation.

IV

EVERY time Rik conferred with potential backers he carried a briefcase swollen with documents and reports concerning the Gruen Watch Company. He visited Burton Joseph, Robert Miller, Lorence Silverberg, Melvin Unterman, and dozens of others. He spent long hours with each of them.

The documents in his briefcase were not half as persuasive as Rik himself. He had studied the Gruen situation thoroughly. He could answer every question, supply every figure. He was able to show that if Gruen changed its management policies — that is, if it fulfilled its present government contracts and undertook no others — its return to the watch business could be highly profitable. He could also show the advantages of selling the Swiss plant, thus raising $5,000,000 in cash through an investment of only $1,500,000, then using the new cash to expand Gruen's interests to other profitable areas.

As for the watches, they could be contracted for at other Swiss factories. There was nothing unusual in this procedure. Several firms in the industry had long operated that way.

All these arguments, plus the reputation Rik had acquired for steering his clients into successful ventures, now prevailed. Yet there was something more than effective argument. As one

49

of the investors later said, "The man had a touch of magic in his enthusiasm. When he talked figures, you followed him — and his pencil — in a kind of hypnosis. His mathematics were incontrovertible. How can you dispute numbers that *show* you will get, among other assets, a $5,000,000 factory by investing $1,500,000?"

Not only did several men come into the new syndicate, but Burton Joseph, alone, subscribed to *three* shares at $50,000 each.

Was it only Rik's persuasiveness that attracted support? Or was there something else? I put this question to one of the men who had followed him into the Gruen deal. He thought about it, then asked, "Am I going to be quoted?"

"Not by name if you prefer it that way."

"For reasons you will see, I *would* like to have my name omitted. On that condition I can tell you a few things which never appeared in financial reports. But they helped Rik form his syndicate."

What he told me was this:

"You must understand the kind of community we had in Minneapolis. Many of us were moderately well-to-do; we had money to invest. But none of us was so outstandingly rich as to think or operate in the millions. Our principal source of income was, as a rule, a family business. Some of us owned retail stores. Some had automobile service stations. Some were in the grain business. Some operated restaurants or movie theaters or drug stores or insurance agencies. In short, we were, for the most part, in what the government classifies as Small Business.

"Now along comes a fellow like Rik. He talks to us about taking over control of a world-famous Big Business like Gruen.

50

He says that assuming control means we in the Minneapolis syndicate — some of us, anyway — will have to become active members of Gruen's board of directors. As a matter of fact, he was candidly saying he'd like to have Burton Joseph as chairman of the Gruen board. I do not want to suggest that this was a determining factor in Burton's making the investment. Burton was too intelligent a businessman to be swayed by anything except the basic prospects of a deal.

"But consider the rest of us. We had the same human frailty or vanity you can find in any average group of men. How do you think I felt, for instance, when I saw the prospect of becoming a director of the Gruen Watch Company? It would be like stepping out on the national financial scene. It would certainly do me no harm in a business way to have the Minneapolis newspapers report I'd been elected to Gruen's board. And socially it would be something of a triumph, too.

"Also, of course, there was the unspoken prospect of getting Gruen business. If you were selling, say, insurance and you were a Gruen director, wouldn't there be a good chance of writing Gruen policies? Or if you were in advertising, might you not hope to get the substantial Gruen account?"

In any case, the syndicate ultimately pledged $750,000 in cash and gave Rik the right to borrow another $750,000 if this became necessary to acquire control of the Gruen Company.

For himself he entered into a peculiar arrangement with his associates. He made no financial investment. His contribution to the syndicate would be the acumen and the labor of negotiating the deal. For this he would receive the first $100,000 in profits accruing to the syndicate; and he would be hired at a salary of $25,000 a year — plus an additional $25,000 for expenses — to manage Gruen's program of expansion and diversification.

Rik was content. Everybody was content.

Negotiations consumed so much of his time, often in Cincinnati, that he could be of little service to Piper, Jaffray, and Hopwood. He resigned from the firm now; he had already resigned from the Hebrew school. Later Palmer Jaffray said, "He had been doing so well as a customers' man that he could have remained with us for life. But we all knew, even before the Gruen deal, that Rik wouldn't spend many years as a securities salesman. His plans and ambitions were bound to carry him away from us. We were sorry to see him go, but we appreciated the inevitability of it."

Eventually the many meetings of lawyers, accountants, bankers, real estate experts and the rest (with all of whom Rik worked closely) resulted in a series of amicable agreements. The Gruen stocks were bought and duly transferred. The Minneapolis syndicate became the controlling group in the watch company.

As Rik had hoped, Burton Joseph was elected chairman of the board, and others of the syndicate joined Joseph at the directors' table. Almost the first order of business for the sixteen directors was to find an experienced, hard-driving executive. Not a single member of the new board, including Rik himself, had any experience in marketing watches. As one director put it, "We needed a wizard."

Rik was ready for this problem. He had been seeking a new president for months, ever since he had started the negotiations for Gruen. Having weighed the qualifications of numerous candidates, he had decided the man who could best preside over Gruen's new bid for success was the former vice-president of the Bulova Watch Company, Edward Weitzen. Weitzen had led Bulova's sales to remarkable heights. Later he had accepted an executive position with the American Machine and Foundry Company, where he was earning $75,000 a year. Moreover, he was of Rik's own generation, a brilliant young man of only thirty-five, and Rik was confident he had found somebody who would talk his own business language. The board agreed.

Rik went to Weitzen with the offer of the Gruen presidency. When he heard what Weitzen was earning, he said, "All right. We'll make it $100,000 a year." (He has frequently remarked, "Why haggle over a few thousand when you're out to make millions?") Weitzen may have been stunned. He said he wanted time to think it over.

"Naturally," Rik agreed. "But think in terms of starting with us by January."

In January 1956, Edward Weitzen became Gruen's president.

Weitzen's talks with Meshulam Riklis certainly apprised him of what Rik planned to do. Nevertheless when the new president settled at his desk and studied the Gruen Company's prospects at close range, he shook his head. He found himself disagreeing with almost every Riklis plan.

For one thing, Weitzen saw no reason to drop future government contracts. For another, he refused to sell the Swiss factory which was to have produced $5,000,000. He wanted Gruen to continue manufacturing its own watches rather than contract for them with others.

Rik could scarcely believe what he heard Weitzen say at the board meeting. He argued. He summoned every fact and figure he could to support the expansion and diversification program he had in mind. The board of directors — no doubt with a sense of embarrassment — found itself compelled to decide whether it would back Rik or Edward Weitzen.

The new president was positive Gruen could earn most profits by remaining in the watch business — by promoting it — by refusing to waste its energies in by-paths. Rik still insisted that the truly big earnings lay in expanding, in acquiring other firms.

Disagreement led to bickering on the board. Bickering led to heated quarrels.

"The weakness of Rik's position," one of the directors later explained, "was that he saw the Gruen Company only as a lever, a means of acquiring other companies. He had no impassioned interest in watches *per se,* even in Gruen *per se* — or so it appeared to Weitzen and many of the board members. Worst of all, Rik could not solidify his arguments by pointing to long years of experience in business. By contrast the strength of Weitzen was that he had *proved* himself an astute merchant during his years with Bulova. He knew watches. He knew the market. His arguments *did* stem from merchandising experience."

The directors disputed and put off decisions for months. By May, however, they could no longer procrastinate. They met in a strained atmosphere. The long-deferred vote had to be cast.

"Gentlemen," said the chairman, "what is your decision?"

Of the sixteen directors at the table twelve — including Board Chairman Burton Joseph — voted with Weitzen. Only four supported the man who had brought Weitzen to Gruen.

2

Twice in his life Meshulam Riklis has suffered a major defeat — or what looked like one. This was the first of those occasions.

He came home a beaten man. Since he had no personal investment in Gruen, no position except that of a hired executive whose methods and counsel had been rejected, he saw only one course to take. He resigned.

Only his closest friends knew how deeply he was hurt by the board's failure to support him. He was now forced to start over again from scratch if he was to pursue the dream of creating an industrial empire.

"I've got to get away for a while," he said. "I need a mental rest."

As it happened, his wife had taken the children to visit her family in Israel. Rik cabled Judy to meet him in Rome. He wanted to travel, to forget Minneapolis and Gruen. He and Judy had sometime earlier celebrated their first five years in the United States by becoming American citizens; so nothing stood in the way of their being abroad. They met late in May, traveled and rested in Europe, and did not return to Minneapolis until the end of summer.

(This must be said: The Gruen Watch Company never recovered from its decline. Eventually Edward Weitzen departed, and the men who had backed him lost a considerable amount of money when they disposed of their holdings. Almost ten years later I discussed the affair with the Joseph brothers in Minneapolis. I asked if their loss had left them bitter against Riklis. Burton answered, "Of course not. *We* were the ones who turned down his plan. We have nobody to blame for that except ourselves. We now feel — in fact, we have known for years — that if we had followed Rik he might have made Gruen the keystone of the empire he later built. Instead we had to stand by and see what he did with Rapid-American. None of us is so foolish as to hold Rik accountable for our own error of judgment. He certainly did *his* best to steer us his way."

This magnanimous appraisal of an unfortunate situation was echoed by other members of the Gruen syndicate. When I asked one of them if he would ever invest with Rik again, he smiled and said, "I already have.")

It would be inaccurate to suggest that Rik used the months in Europe merely to lick his wounds. He has always had the optimistic faculty of looking forward, not backward. Almost every man of active mind has been too impatient to waste time on recriminations, and Rik is no exception. Too resilient to snap under tension, by the time he had been in Europe a week he was planning what he would do on his return to America.

"The setback with Gruen," he said on one occasion, "showed me clearly that next time I must not be content with being a member of a group, merely *advising* it on negotiations and acquisitions. I must *lead* the group. I must be responsible for the daily management of its affairs."

Another thing too was clear. To his next backers he had to present stronger arguments for following a course of acquisitions and mergers. He had to make its importance compelling, convincing, attractive. And he had many valid and original points to offer.

They were original because, in that summer of 1956, brokers were not yet discussing such matters very widely. Rik could see that the advantages of mergers must be as applicable to sellers as to buyers; if a merger did not benefit both parties, it would be pointless. For himself, however, he was approaching the problem from the *buyer's* point of view. I can count off at least ten items that might be persuasive:

1. It is much easier and quicker to acquire an existing source of income — a going business — than to develop a new one. (This is a fact Rik has never ceased to stress. In later years when he bought the McCrory-McLellan-Green stores, the Otasco chain and others, he acquired 1,300 retail outlets. How long would it have taken to *establish* such a chain of variety stores, and how much would it have cost? Similarly, when his Rapid-American Corporation purchased the Joseph H. Cohen and Sons Company, it bought an eighty-year-old firm that was grossing $45,000,000 a year and showing an annual profit of over $4,000,000. Would it have been possible to build a new business of such proportions in the six months that were required to negotiate the deal?)

2. One could argue that to merge for purposes of diversifying a company's interests is, in essence, a purchase of insurance. If one area of sales declines, the parent company can remain vigorous and solvent through the productivity of its other divisions.

3. One could demonstrate how feasible it is to apply a subsidiary's losses against a corporation's current and future earnings. Not that this can be the sole or avowed reason for a merger; the Internal Revenue Service would quickly say no. But if it turns out to be an *added* benefit in an amalgamation that has other positive features, it is permissible — and obviously a way to save corporate tax money.

4. Acquiring another firm can be the swiftest, most direct way of coming into possession of profitable new product lines,

new patents and trademarks. It is, moreover, a shortcut to enjoying the fruits of long research and development done by someone else. And it can mean the immediate acquisition of the good will — and the market — created by long years of advertising and service on the part of the purchased firm. Who can deny the importance of such advantages?

5. To buy a company can include buying the services of its management. The most successful merger-makers are those who retain the executive ability of former owners on long-term, generous contracts. Who, they reason, can run a business better than the men who built it, the men who understand all its problems?

6. What is true of managerial services is equally true of technical knowledge. The merger can bring to the parent company the kind of experienced technical sophistication one can rarely find in the open market.

7. "Vertical mergers" — those in which a corporation seeks to save money by acquiring its primary sources of raw materials or its own avenues of distribution — have merits so obvious that it is futile to question them. Apart from resulting in savings, they assure efficient distribution of products.

8. Unquestionably, one could point out, the joining of many resources provides a broader basis for credit to every division of the combined companies. Thus it promotes the possibility of expansion and development. How much more practical and intelligent it is, from a business point of view, to belong to a large complex which commands a credit line of $50,000,000 than to a small one which finds it difficult to raise even $1,000,000!

9. Then there is what is sometimes termed "the pressure of cash." A company may find itself with an excessive amount of

reserve funds. This may be the result of having had to liquidate some of its divisions. Or there may have been what is
known as a "heavy internal cash flow" which cannot be rein-
vested in the company's own facilities; these may already be
adequate for all foreseeable needs. What then is to be done
with the excessive cash? How can it be used to better advantage than by employing it to effect a merger which will add to
the corporation's security, giving it a wider diversification of
activities?

10. And always, of course, there is the perfectly normal,
human satisfaction of having a *big* operation rather than a
small one. This may well be the primary motive of many an
entrepreneur in the merger field.

All these facts and many more were no doubt part of Rik's
armament when he returned from Europe. He came home re-
freshed, as confident as ever that the dream circles he had
once drawn could be converted to realities.

Once more he turned to the proxy statements, the annual
reports, the balance sheets of firms represented on the board
of the Cincinnati Stock Exchange. This had been the source of
Marion, of Balcrank, of Gruen. He was in the midst of this
search when he received a telephone call from a Cincinnati
broker named Fred Korros. This was the man through whom
he had learned much about his former Cincinnati deals; and
Rik had a sound respect for Korros's judgment.

Now Korros spoke about a new "situation." Rik listened
without comment, then asked to see the company's balance
sheets and other documents. When they arrived he studied
them — and abruptly discovered that this was a corporation
whose status excited him.

It was called the Rapid Electrotype Company.

3

Rapid Electrotype was by no means a small firm. As a manufacturer of electrotype plates and related products, it ranked second in the nation. Nor was it wholly a local enterprise. Its five big plants were scattered throughout the country. In the year before it was brought to Rik's attention, Rapid's sales had been approximately $4,200,000; its profits had run to $300,000.

But what really focused his eyes on the company was this: it had $1,600,000 of liquid assets — cash or its equivalent — which could be acquired with the purchase. The 123,784 outstanding shares of its stock were in very few hands, a large block of them belonging to the company's aging head, Peter Schotanus. So negotiations would be reasonably concentrated; and the shares were selling at $18.

Of course, Rik would have to pay more. One of the strongest inducements in any such transaction is to offer the owner of securities more than he can possibly raise in any other way — enough to make him view the price as a kind of bonanza or personal triumph or, at the very least, a vindication of his judgment in selling.

Rik studied the Rapid Electrotype Company's position thoroughly. He went to see its plants. The more he saw the more certain he became that this would be a solid base from which to build for the future.

Armed with all he had learned, he went to interview Rapid's chief executive officer and largest shareholder, Peter Schotanus. Mr. Schotanus must have been surprised by the youth of the man who offered to buy his 10 per cent of the company. Possibly he was disconcerted, too, by the fact that Rik had no knowledge whatever of the electrotype business or of anything even remotely connected with it. Ordinarily such factors might have induced Schotanus to wave this proposition aside as absurd.

What checked the refusal was, first of all, the fact that Rik was offering $28 per share, almost $10 more than Rapid's market price. Second, Fred Korros was in effect sponsoring Rik (it was Korros who had arranged this meeting) and the financial community of Cincinnati respected Korros. Third, one of the city's largest and richest investors — a friend and client of Korros — was Lionel Rosenbaum, a man whose nod of approbation was a kind of pontifical blessing. Rik had met Rosenbaum's son Jay at college; they had become friends; and now Lionel Rosenbaum had only to say, "Yes, Rik is a friend of my son's" to create a positive impression on Peter Schotanus.

After several meetings with the young man from Minneapolis, and after hours of friendly, low-keyed discussion at each of these conferences, Peter Schotanus decided that yes, perhaps at seventy he had reached that stage of life at which he might well consider selling his Rapid holdings.

He and Rik shook hands. As he rose, Rik knew his hardest job was about to begin.

Ideally it might have been wise to aim for 51 per cent of the outstanding Rapid stock, thus winning undisputed control of the company. But Rik saw that it was possible to assume a controlling position with less than a majority. Besides, he was not at all sure at this point — after the Gruen debacle — that he could raise the million and a half or so it would take to acquire a 51 per cent interest.

Taking account of his personal resources, he found that they now amounted to about $25,000. And this time he was determined to possess a share in his own syndicate, not to be merely its hired man and adviser. With this in mind he set out again to talk to Minneapolis investors. Now he could say, *"I'm investing $25,000."*

In a matter of weeks he was able to raise $400,000 from a group which included a number of people who had joined him in the past. Men like Mel Unterman, Lorence Silverberg, Robert Miller and others had unshakable faith in him.

Using the $400,000, Rik set out to buy Rapid securities on margin — and he crashed into unexpected opposition.

One of Rapid's newer stockholders, Jerome K. Jelin, objected to letting Rapid's control pass into the hands of the Minneapolis syndicate. Jelin's attorney, Harry Wachtel of New York, wrote Rik that his client would fight this so-termed "take-over" to the finish.

Rik was amazed. He had not anticipated such objections. After all, he was offering far more than the market price of Rapid stock. He hesitated, for Jelin's attitude was challenging one of his own basic principles — that a deal, to be good, must please both sides; that to engage in a vicious proxy fight is seldom worth the anger and resentment it stirs. Again and again in later years Rik "walked away," as he put it, from deals that promised well until he found that large blocks of voting stock were opposed to a merger. He has never engaged in such proxy fights. He might have walked away from Rapid, too — except for two considerations.

First, Jelin was virtually alone in his opposition, and his holdings represented only a small percentage of the company's securities.

Second, Rik had already raised the enthusiasm of his syndicate to so high a level that he could hardly let it collapse because of one man's opposition.

He decided to press on in spite of Jelin's objections. Jelin's lawyer, Harry Wachtel, fought the "take-over" in every possible way. He marshaled every law, every device, every delaying tactic he could think of, and the arguments he presented in meetings with Rik, with Schotanus, with Korros, with bankers and brokers and other stockholders, were unquestionably strong and brilliant. But they did not prevent the Minneapolis syndicate from acquiring some 30,000 shares of Rapid stock.

This was so powerful a holding that it resulted in winning for the group half the seats on Rapid's board of directors. Except for the Jelin contest, the deal had been negotiated in so friendly a way, with never a hint of pressure on anyone, that the new board, sitting around its table, found no difficulty in adopting a spirit of cooperation.

No one disputed the fact that this new setup was the result of Rik's own efforts; and no one could doubt that Rik's plans for the future, so full of enthusiasm and mathematical persuasiveness, could lead Rapid to a new era of prosperity. Once the board began to recognize and accept his leadership in the enterprise, the outcome was inevitable.

In November directors of the Rapid Electrotype Company elected Meshulam Riklis, not quite thirty-two years old, their chairman and chief executive officer.

For the first time in his life he now held corporate power. He was in a position to lead his associates into the kind of empire-building he had so long envisioned. One of the first steps he took was to move Rapid's headquarters to New York. This was the arena of Big Business.

He brought his family to Long Island and urged four of his

close associates — Miller, Unterman, Silverberg and Divine — to join him. The power of his persuasiveness can be judged from the fact that all four moved their families to New York in order to become Rapid officers!

Rik had hardly settled down in his new office when he put in a telephone call to lawyer Harry Wachtel. "Though we were on opposite sides of the fence," he told Wachtel, "I couldn't help admiring the way you handled your side of the case. You did a wonderful job. I like the way you think and act. I want to retain you for Rapid."

"In what capacity?" Wachtel asked.

"I'm asking you to become Rapid's co-counsel. You'll work with our present lawyer who's in Minneapolis."

That was in 1956. Harry Wachtel wanted time to think. He had to be sure that this association would involve no conflict of interests.

In the end Wachtel accepted the offer. He began as a kind of consultant. In time he became chief counsel — and he is still the head of the corporation's legal arm.

In the light of what has happened during the years since 1956, this can be regarded as the real start of Meshulam Riklis's climb to billion-dollar eminence. There were to be as many setbacks in the future as there had been in the past. He was to know the pain of defeat — indeed, of near tragedy — as well as the elation of triumph. As philosophers have pointed out through the centuries, for all of us there is just as much downhill as uphill in this world.

V

USUALLY a discussion of mergers must be simplified, even oversimplified, if it is to be comprehensible to the person whose training does not include law, accountancy, real estate, banking, stockbrokerage, and several other highly specialized financial disciplines. The record of one major merger, for instance, may include scores of phrases like:

Deferred maintenance
Certificate of necessity
Preferred par
FIFO (first-in-first-out)
Pure interest
Protective covenants

A layman may be able to define several such terms, but can he clearly grasp the significance of them all? Can he interpret the meaning of a statement like: "8 per cent is the capitalization rate implicit in a price-earnings ratio of 20.12 when earnings per share are expected to grow for 10 years at an annual rate of 6.5 per cent"?

When I spoke of this with a senior partner of a stockbrokerage firm, he maintained that anybody truly interested in mergers *would* understand the terms involved. They were common enough in financial parlance, he argued.

I knew this broker was engaged in negotiations with a pharmaceutical firm which was seeking financial support. A prospectus that the company had prepared lay on his desk. I leafed through it while waiting for him to finish a telephone conversation. Now I picked it up again and suggested that his own "true interest" in the pharmaceutical firm surely made him familiar with its terminology.

He nodded. "I have to know what they're talking about, yes."

In that case, I asked, could he define some of the words that baffled me on the very first page of the prospectus. I read only three terms:

Bendroflumethiazine

Methenamine mandelate

Busolfan

He was silent. After a moment he sighed. "All right," he said. "Every man to his own specialty. You probably *will* have to simplify if you want to be understood."

The truth is that in mergers we deal with one of the most complex of financial procedures. It is easy enough to report that on a certain date Meshulam Riklis of Rapid-American and the head of another corporation shook hands and agreed that their companies would merge. Such an agreement is not the termination of anything. It is only a *beginning*. From that moment on, other people have to plunge into the task of bringing all the elements of a possible merger into harmony — and in compliance with countless laws and regulations.

The documents that were necessary to conclude the merger of Rapid-American and one of its largest acquisitions total several thousand pages. They are bound in two volumes, each three inches thick. They represent the result of negotiations that took almost a year to coordinate and complete. I have seen men come out of such meetings in utter exhaustion.

What does this plethora of documents consist of? It includes the financial statements of both corporations, the detailed statements of their subsidiary organizations, the opinions of attorneys, the minutes of meetings, the methods of payment or of exchanging securities, the resolutions adopted by both boards of directors, the letters of explanation to stockholders (detailing the benefits of the merger) as well as requests for stockholder support and proxies. In fact, the very index of the documents involved covers several pages.

So, whenever I say that Meshulam Riklis brought about the merger of Rapid-American with some other corporation, I hope no one will forget that such an accomplishment represents the work of many committees and many individuals; that a single printed phrase like "the merger was completed on such-and-such a date" reflects long months of arduous work on the part of experts in every area of modern finance and industry.

If one reads in the press that negotiations for a certain merger or acquisition have been delayed or abandoned, it is usually because some of the individual negotiators have been unable to reach agreements in their own areas of interest. To illustrate: At a time when the stock market is undergoing violent fluctuations it becomes extremely difficult to agree on specific terms for exchanging one corporation's securities for another's. At what daily rate shall the exchange be pegged when values are changing from hour to hour? And if two parties disagree on the future prospects of their companies, is it possible to complete a valuation as it may be a year away?

Another important question: How can the representatives of

67

banks being asked to finance a deal agree on terms when they cannot even fix the current value of the shares being offered as collateral?

Even the simplest of mergers develops individual and often complicated problems. When Riklis set out to add a soft-goods division to Rapid-American, his acquisition of the Merry Mites Company and the Hi-Line Company was a comparatively smooth operation. It involved payment in 30,124 shares of Rapid-American common stock. One would say, on glancing through the record, that all went well.

Yet there was an obstacle which all but halted negotiations. The seller wished to be guaranteed reimbursement for any sums he might have to pay as the result of pending suits for trademark infringement. He felt certain he would win the cases. Nevertheless he wanted protection. How far could Rapid-American commit itself in assuming such an obligation?

Also, the seller insisted on having Rapid-American contribute 15 per cent of its payroll to a bonus plan for his employees. And for himself he asked a five-year contract at $50,000 a year.

The two latter stipulations could be met easily enough; they represented specific amounts of money. But the first one, eventually compromised, consumed many long conferences since nobody could foretell how much would be involved.

No, nothing is simple in concluding a merger. The astonishing thing about men like Meshulam Riklis — about Rik above most others, I suspect — is that they are experts in every aspect of consummating a merger. They seem to know more law than lawyers, more accountancy than accountants.

A Certified Public Accountant, an able and experienced man, told me of the report he had once prepared for Rik. "My staff and I worked on it for weeks," he said. "It was a matter that involved many millions of dollars. When at last I placed a two-hundred-page document on Mr. Riklis's desk, he turned at once to the last page of the summary. He glanced at it for hardly thirty seconds, then told me, 'You've made a mistake. These figures can't be right.'

"I assured him they had to be right. Six accountants had taken over a month to make sure of every figure. But Riklis insisted that we check back over the entire report. I was indignant. He was challenging my accuracy on the basis of a single glance. Nevertheless, in spite of my fuming, I took the report and checked again.

"A few days later I went back to Riklis's office, and this time I was shamefaced. When I put the papers on his desk the figures were different. He had been right. He looked at the final sheet, nodded, and said, 'Good.' That was all. No criticism of the mistake we had made. No sign of self-satisfaction in having been right. He was as unemotional about the figures as an electronic computer."

He *had* to be cool, unruffled, almost machinelike. For immediately after becoming board chairman of the Rapid Electrotype Company he found himself considering one expansion possibility after another which demanded clear-minded judgment and planning.

At the same time he undertook an inspection trip of all Rapid plants. When he met the managers it was to offer them the kind of incentives they had never had before. They were to share in profits. They were to receive stock options. Their employees were to enjoy a pension plan beyond anything that had ever previously been offered to them.

Rik may not have known much about electrotype, but he

understood how people would respond to profit sharing. His offers resulted in new enthusiasm for Rapid's entire staff — and a 50 per cent increase in profits that first year!

Now, with a solid platform from which to operate, his thinking expanded. Where would he turn next? He could see, for instance, that there was an exciting industrial future in electronic data processing. In fact, he was confident that data processing would soon be earning millions.

To get into that field he felt he needed a company already manufacturing office equipment, preferably typewriters. These, he maintained, were the very basis of many data processing projects.

In his search for "situations" he had met one investor, the renowned Gurdon Wattles, who owned about 20 per cent of the Smith-Corona Typewriter Company. The company's reputation was excellent. In truth, it was *so* good that when Rik mentioned his hopes to his associates he might as well have said, "I want to buy General Motors."

One of them asked, "Why should Wattles want to sell Smith-Corona?"

"Why *shouldn't* he?" Rik countered. "If the price is right. I plan to offer him $1,500,000 for his 20 per cent interest."

He had studied the latest Smith-Corona balance sheet. The company had $1,500,000 in cash, $5,800,000 in accounts receivable, about $10,600,000 in inventories — total assets of some $18,000,000. In addition there was the attraction of plants worth $7,300,000 and other properties, not to mention the considerable value of the company's good will.

What interested Rik as much as the company's reputation and balance sheet were three factors he listed in this order:

1. Smith-Corona had a small capitalization of about 300,000 shares.
2. Its book value was greater than its market value.
3. Its earnings were impressive, "though erratic."

Rik went to see Gurdon Wattles. Mr. Wattles was always willing to listen to a proposal. Possibly, like so many others, he concealed a smile when the very young Meshulam Riklis came into his office. But when Rik started talking Mr. Wattles stopped smiling. You don't deprecate somebody who comes in to give you $1,500,000. (Rik's offer was supported, of course, by the assets of Rapid Electrotype.)

The upshot of several meetings was that Mr. Wattles sold his Smith-Corona holdings to Rapid Electrotype.

Riklis knew that the typewriter company had recently rejected an opportunity to buy an electronic firm, Kleinschmidt Laboratories, which was manufacturing teletype machines. Yet he also knew that this kind of acquisition could lead directly into the data processing area. Despite Smith-Corona's former reluctance to buy the Kleinschmidt Laboratories, he made investigations of his own. As he reported to the Rapid board:

"I was deeply impressed with this company's potential growth, by its able management, good facilities, and its possible coordination with Smith-Corona. Even the $2,300,000 being asked by Kleinschmidt seems reasonable for a company earning between $600,000 and $800,000 after taxes."

He took his case to the Smith-Corona board. He must have been as persuasive here as he had been with his syndicate in Minneapolis, for Smith-Corona, reconsidering its previous decision, now voted — in May of 1956 — to acquire Kleinschmidt.

This was Smith-Corona's first move toward diversification. Spurred by the future potentialities of the combined enterprises — surely a natural combination for operations in the data processing field — Rik urged Rapid's board to buy more Smith-Corona stock. And the purchases continued until Rapid owned approximately 40 per cent of Smith-Corona.

This proved to be a mistake.

Suddenly the Smith-Corona management saw its control being threatened by the incursion of outsiders. Lawyers and directors hurriedly met to plan a defense. They found it in the idea of buying Kleinschmidt with 80,000 shares of Smith-Corona stock instead of with cash, as originally agreed.

This meant that there would now be over 400,000 shares of Smith-Corona stock outstanding. In consequence Rapid's portion would be diluted. It would represent only 30 per cent of the outstanding securities — a tremendous reduction of strength. Moreover, Smith-Corona further reduced Rapid's influence by placing another block of securities — about 20 per cent of the total — on the market.

Rik came nearer to anger then than any of his associates had ever before seen him. He went to court, seeking to prevent the Smith-Corona action. A referee rejected his appeal.

Meeting with the directors of Rapid Electrotype, Rik told them: "The only solution is a proxy fight, and that would be a waste of energy. Besides, I see no reason for staying where we are not wanted. And it is obvious that Smith-Corona does *not* want us. I recommend that we get rid of our Smith-Corona stock and turn our attention to more attractive areas."

By September, only a few months after the securities had been purchased, Rapid sold its Smith-Corona holdings — and emerged from the experience with a rewarding profit.

For whatever the facts are worth, the Smith-Corona management was dismissed within a year. The Kleinschmidt management took over its operations.

By that time Rik had transferred his attention to other possibilities. Had he learned anything new from the Smith-Corona experience? "I learned," he said, "that a controlling interest in a company must be affirmed *by a majority representation on its board of directors.*"

In other words, if he was to direct the destinies of the firms he acquired, it was essential to place on their boards men who understood and would support his aims.

Clearly the thirty-two-year-old Meshulam Riklis was being toughened by the realities of the market place. This was his mood when he turned his consideration to the company which was eventually to supply the other half in the hyphenated name of the Rapid-American Corporation.

It was the American Colortype Company.

2

Gurdon Wattles, from whom Rik had purchased 125,000 shares of Smith-Corona, was the man who broached the matter of American Colortype. This occurred even before Rapid had disposed of its Smith-Corona stock. Mr. Wattles owned about 50 per cent of American Colortype's 250,000 shares. He was ready to sell his holdings for $4,500,000.

What was American Colortype? In its three principal divisions it was a printing company, a greeting card manufacturer, a metal-sign maker. It had a book value of $12,000,000.

Wattles's 125,000 shares needed only 1 per cent more of the corporation's securities — about 2,500 shares — to assure indisputable control. It should not be difficult to pick this up on the open market.

What attracted Rik most strongly was the fact that American Colortype had $1,300,000 in cash, $4,900,000 in accounts receivable, over $4,000,000 in inventories. These added up to immediate assets of over $10,000,000 which could be controlled by the investment of half that sum! In addition, of course, American Colortype owned plants and real estate worth about $5,000,000. These could be liquidated to generate cash.

Obviously it was the kind of deal which had all the advantages Rik regarded as his criteria for making acquisitions.

Rapid Electrotype purchased Gurdon Wattles's holdings for the $4,500,000 that had been asked, and of this 60 per cent was paid in cash; the balance was due in six months.

How could it pay $4,500,000? Where was the money obtained?

In Rik's own words: "To make the first payment on the deal we borrowed $1,000,000 from a bank and sold $1,600,000 of convertible debentures.

"I intended merging Rapid Electrotype and American Colortype fast, thus having the credit of *both* companies to back the second payment if it was necessary to borrow money. But this final payment coincided with our sale in September of the Smith-Corona stock for about $2,000,000. So there was no money problem. We had what we needed.

"The management of American Colortype was taken over, and we at once set out on a program of cash generation. American Colortype's real estate and some other assets were quickly sold. In this way it took only four months to generate close to $6,000,000 in cash.

"So, you see, we were doing well. Though we owed $1,000,000 to the bank we controlled 51 per cent of American Colortype, which in turn now had over $6,000,000 in cash."

The neat dovetailing of events — having the sale of Smith-Corona stock produce $2,000,000 in time to meet the final payment for American Colortype stock — was not a wholly unplanned coincidence. When Riklis agreed to pay Gurdon Wattles the 40 per cent still due him ($1,800,000) in six months, he had set the date far enough ahead to *allow* for the money-raising sale of the Smith-Corona holdings.

This early transaction helps to explain why in later years he came to be regarded as a master at timing. Again and again he has scheduled events for what developed to be the most propitious moments to insure their success.

Have these things happened by coincidence? By luck? The facts too often deny the element of chance. At board meetings Rik has frequently described what he planned to accomplish in the next year or two. He has resorted to chalkboard talks like a professor outlining a theorem. And somehow his schedules generally work out as predicted.

Certainly this was the case when the Rapid Electrotype Company prepared to merge with American Colortype to form the Rapid-American Corporation. Preparation meant, in large part, acquiring more and more American Colortype stock, till he had full control.

He was so confident of the future that he signed a long-term lease for an entire floor of offices at 711 Fifth Avenue.

"Do we really need all this expensive space?" one of the directors asked as he passed uneasily from office to office.

"You can't play in the big leagues," Rik answered, "unless you have a big league park."

So, a board chairman at the age of thirty-three and the father of three children (there was now a son, Ira), Meshulam Riklis looked out at the world from behind a huge Fifth Avenue desk. At his elbow there were two telephones. In the outer office sat his new secretary, Mrs. Mary Friedwald, and her assistant. In other offices were the men he had gathered about him as his immediate staff, for the most part those who had followed from Minneapolis.

He was entrenched. His dream of an industrial empire at last had a base from which to expand.

Part Two

THE YEARS OF GROWTH

VI

EVER since Budd Schulberg wrote *What Makes Sammy Run?* the same questions have been asked about many of our most dynamic businessmen. What makes them keep pressing so hard? What is the inexhaustible source of their energy? What are their motivations? In short, what kind of men build today's fortunes?

Some answers are intriguing. Some are incisive and shrewd. Yet none I have ever heard has been wholly satisfying. Nobody can present every facet of a person in a single reply.

Almost every successful man one reads about is pictured as flamboyant, self-centered, reckless in his rush to snatch at his next million. Some are called arrogant, some impatient, and virtually all eccentric. For example, in Chris Welles's study of another merger-maker (one I first heard mentioned as "a younger Riklis") *Life* magazine said:

"Charles Bluhdorn's business and obsession is buying other people's businesses — any kind of business, from a $5,000,000 auto-bumper manufacturer to an $83,000,000 zinc miner. . . . Bluhdorn plunges after his prospects with the passion of a storefront evangelist. On the telephone he makes flowery speeches to businessmen he hasn't even met, describing the great blessings that will follow if they join forces with Bluhdorn. When he meets a prospect Bluhdorn cosily drapes an arm around his neck and, lips close to the prospect's ear, murmurs, 'You and I are going to make a hell of a team.' But let the prospect waver and draw back and a terrible change comes over Bluhdorn. His face darkens, his chin juts, his hands flail the air, and his voice rises to a roar of anger and disappointment. 'How can you turn down a deal like this?' he demands. 'You're crazy!'

"Actually a lot of people on Wall Street think Bluhdorn is the one who's crazy. 'The Mad Austrian,' they call him. . . . All he wants to do, all he ever talks about, is to get bigger faster than anyone else, reaching a billion in sales in two years, then two billion. 'People say this can't be done,' he says. 'Well, that is the best way of convincing me to do it.'"

I have sought traces of this kind of drive in Riklis. They simply do not exist — at least, they do not exist visibly.

Rik's color lies in the very antithesis of flamboyance. He is so utterly calm, so quiet and reserved, that one wonders if he *ever* raises his voice. This man who once wore pink shirts to business meetings has become one of the best-tailored figures in New York — trim and conservative in attire, given to dark suits, showing a touch of gray at his temples to lend dignity to his chairman-of-the-board status. He has a quiet, ready smile, an air of complete relaxation. In all that has ever been said or written about him I have found nothing that suggests a wild temperament.

So I have accepted the fact that though we may speak of certain individuals as tycoons or financiers or capitalists, that is about as far as we can generalize. There is no way of applying the same descriptives to, say, a Norton Simon who acquires McCall's; to a Henry Ford who acquires Philco; to

I. T. & T.'s Harold S. Geneen; and to Meshulam Riklis. Each
has his own philosophy, his own ambitions, his own pace. I
have come to suspect that there is only one common characteristic among them all — *determination.*

Some show resolution by the use of raw power. They are the
fighters. They are willing to fight for proxies and for the de-
struction of all opposition. And they are proud of their toughness.

Meshulam Riklis, on the other hand, prefers the diplomatic
way. He never uses a club. He relies on logic, on persuasiveness, on a friendly approach.

Somewhere in the depths of his mind there must be a love
of showmanship, too. For he has demonstrated time after time
how much he likes to rely on dramatic improvisation.

For instance, when Rik speaks of the methods by which he
financed the acquisition of American Colortype he says
merely, "We borrowed a million dollars from a bank."

How did he borrow a million dollars?

What prompted the bankers to give so large a sum to a
virtually unknown young foreigner? Bernard Gerald Cantor,
the investment banker and one of Rik's close associates, accompanied him when he went to seek the loan. Cantor reports the
incident this way:

"I could not understand why Rik wanted to do business
with the officers of this particular bank. They had the reputation of being anti-Semitic. I had been told they had little to do
with Jewish firms unless they were old, solidly established,
heavy with cash. I didn't think we had even a slim chance of
getting a million dollars from these people. And I warned Rik
of what to expect. He said only, 'Leave it to me.'

"When we walked into their conference room the two

bankers we had come to see sat tight-lipped. I guessed from their expressions that their minds were made up. They were not going to do business with us.

"We had hardly sat down when Rik said bluntly, 'I hear you boys are anti-Semites.'

"Just like that. Like a punch in the mouth. You could see the two men catch their breath, unable to believe such a frontal attack. I wanted to drop through the floor. I was convinced Rik had ruined every chance we had even of talking with these people.

"They hotly denied the anti-Semitic charge. They defended themselves so convincingly that ever since then I have felt I'd been wrong about them. As the conversation went on I realized we weren't even discussing the money we had come to borrow. The business of our visit seemed to be taken for granted. The important thing was for these men to disprove the charge of anti-Semitism.

"By the time we got around to talking about the million dollars the main barrier between us — the bank's alleged attitude toward Jews — had been removed, and nothing else seemed worth arguing about. They lent us the money.

"When we left the bank Rik gave me a wry smile. 'I'll bet,' he said, 'if I had told you in advance what I was going to do you would have protested.' I answered that I wouldn't even have gone into the bank with him. 'But we got what we came for, didn't we?' he said. 'And we turned those men into friends. So what was wrong with putting it to them straight? I think it was a successful visit.'"

It was indeed, and there is no doubt that Rik enjoyed his triumph. I say this with a purpose. For if anyone were to ask me to prescribe any single rule for success as I have observed it in Riklis, it would be precisely that: *thoroughly to enjoy what one does.*

And what else, besides the joy of conquest, does it take to make millions? First of all, one has to conclude, there is a certain state of mind.

For Rik building a financial empire is life's most exhilarating adventure. As a painter derives pleasure from working on a canvas, as a writer is stirred by creating what may become The Great American Novel, so Rik reacts to the thrill of building a mighty industrial complex. He loves the challenge.

One of his friends says, "For him establishing a business empire is a compulsion. It's the most urgent need of his life. When he couldn't begin with a Gruen, he turned to a Smith-Corona. When it couldn't be Smith-Corona, he turned to something else. The means were never as important as the ultimate target. And he never stops aiming at that target. What's more, it keeps growing bigger and bigger. Once he might have been content with the prospect of building a $50,000,000 empire. Today he is thinking in billions."

Another man put it this way: "He is like a chess player whose sole objective is to win the game. He plans the moves ahead carefully. But he also plans alternate moves. If one fails he is ready with another. What drives a man like him is the *excitement* of the game."

I never dispute such opinions. I merely find each of them inadequate. There are a hundred other explanations that can be made in analyzing the careers of entrepreneurs like Riklis. One that impressed me with its insight came from a member of his board of directors:

"I don't think Rik has ever been awed by big figures. They simply don't faze him. You and I might recoil from the idea of trying to borrow millions of dollars. We would begin by asking ourselves why anybody should *want* to lend us such sums. Not Rik. He asks for millions as confidently as the rest of us might ask for hundreds. To him money is a commodity, a means of building something. Big sums or small, they are all the same. I don't think he cares about money as anything but a tool for getting what he next wants to acquire. It explains why in his first years he did not build a great personal fortune. He concentrated on building the fortunes of his empire."

Young people with bright dreams are forever asking successful businessmen like Rik to provide a formula for achieving wealth. Usually the replies are dismal platitudes. Perhaps because, in a subconscious way, I never wanted to trap Rik into uttering such a cliché I myself never put the question to him.

But there was a day, not long ago, when he addressed the graduate students of the Harvard School of Business Administration. Standing at the lectern of a crowded auditorium, he talked easily and informally of the opportunities the modern economy offers. Some three hundred men listened in a kind of mesmerism, for here was one whose career was proof of his words.

When he finished his speech the first question from the audience was: "Mr. Riklis, what do you consider the most important qualities a man must have today to become a success in business?"

Without hesitation Rik replied, "He must be naive, stupid, crazy, and lazy."

There was a puzzled hush. Somebody uttered an uncertain laugh. Then Rik smiled and explained:

"A man must be naive enough to feel he must share his

success with others and to believe his wildest ambitions are attainable. Stupid enough to discount the experience of those who tell him, 'It can't be done,' and to be sure there must be a way. Crazy enough to persist toward his goal in spite of all obstacles and discouragement. And lazy enough to turn authority and responsibility in important matters over to others — the experts."

I have frequently thought that this was a remarkable bit of self-analysis.

But every balance sheet, whether of a corporation or of a man, must show liabilities as well as assets. What, then, are the liabilities of an entrepreneur like Meshulam Riklis?

"He has the mistaken notion," says one man, "that everybody associated with him shares his ambition to create an enormous empire. There is no doubt that in the long run he will have built an immensely profitable organization for his stockholders. But he obdurately ignores the fact that there are many who would rather sit tight with what they've got so far and take their profits now."

Another points to this fault: "For a long time Rik had a mistaken sense of loyalty. I've seen him keep executives on the job long after they had proved their incompetence — just because they had become his friends. He always seems to hope a man will improve. This kind of loyalty may be admirable if you're running your own private business. But when you head a corporation your responsibility is to thousands of stockholders. Such misplaced loyalty can be costly to investors. Fortunately Rik has learned in recent years to replace poor executives with good ones as fast as necessary. But he still has to battle with himself when a man ought to be fired."

When you have summed up such comments, praise as well

as criticism, you conclude that men like Riklis have the same human frailties, the same dreams and hopes as all of us. But *they* have the strength and the determination to turn dreams into action. And they waste no time in doing it.

"For Rik," one man said, "a new opportunity is like the starter's shot at a track meet. He's instantly off and running at full speed."

Rik's own way of commenting on his operations can be surprisingly simple. Some of the points he makes apply to all entrepreneurs who thrive on making mergers.

"This merger business," he said to a small group of young executives, "is one activity that demands every bit of thought and energy a man can give it. He has to meet a variety of challenges, whether it be in explaining to his own colleagues the advantages of a contemplated deal or in convincing the bankers and financial institutions of the soundness of a project so that they will help finance it.

"Then — and I cannot overstress the importance of this — he has to study the motives and the needs of the party he negotiates with. Negotiations take place *between human beings*. Each has his own problems, his own ways, his own desires. No deal can be successfully consummated without adjusting the terms to fit the seller's needs; nor without taking into account the fact that he will be surrounded by experts and advisers who must also be convinced that the seller is gaining something by the merger.

"There must also be a clear evaluation of the status and conditions of one's own company, the buyer. What is the state of its financial strength? What are its limitations? *How* will it go about bringing a merger to a satisfactory conclusion? With what form of payment? Is the proposed merger to be a tax-free or a taxable transaction? If tax-free, then the issuance of common or preferred stock has to be used instead of cash. If taxable, then cash or deferred payments or a combination of both may be planned. Moreover, there is the question of whether a merger will require a stockholders' vote. All such matters must be settled before any formula can be developed. This is far from a simple business, and I certainly don't recommend it for amateurs unless they are backed by a corps of experts.

"One last point I would like to make," Rik said to the group, "concerns the handling of cash. In our organization the control of the actual cash flow lies in our home office. In that way we can make the most effective use of it. For the holding of cash has two great advantages. First, it commands the confidence, respect, and the good relations with financial institutions without whose support no management can operate effectively; and second, cash creates the ability to expand and make acquisitions *without* the use of hard cash — using cash only as the gauge of our borrowing power."

2

The financial world has become so deeply interested in mergers that for the past few years the American Management Association has been sponsoring periodic seminars on the subject. One of them was conducted by the late Jerome S. Hollender who headed the Mergers and Acquisitions Division of Shearson, Hammill and Company, stockbrokers.

"People fill these seminars," Mr. Hollender said, "as if mergers were a wholly new development in the United States.

Yet there is nothing basically novel about them, except the fact that we now have more than ever before."

Companies that effect mergers, Hollender made clear, have been creating ingenious substitutes for cash — printing their own money, in effect. These substitutes are, as a rule, in the form of newly issued stock which one corporation exchanges for the existing securities of another.

In the eighteen-month period before June 30, 1966, such new stock issues, created for merger purposes (as listed by the New York Stock Exchange) amounted to $3,100,000,000.

This means that in eighteen months merging corporations issued over $3,000,000,000 *in their own "home-made" form of currency!*

These currencies, Jerome Hollender said, include "common stock, convertible or non-convertible preferred stock or bonds and notes, or combinations of these. A specific issue can be created to meet the particular requirements of a transaction."

And he concluded: "An acquisition-minded company should have a full variety of 'currencies' available. This should be authorized *before* it is required for an acquisition in order to permit maximum flexibility in negotiations."

Riklis, like others in the merger field, has made extensive use of every legal method of payment which meets the stipulations of the Securities and Exchange Commission and of other government regulations.

Studying these various forms of acknowledging indebtedness, one begins to suspect that all currency is a man-made illusion. Currency is merely a promise to pay, and it seems to matter little whether this promise is expressed in the form of dollar bills, of debentures, or of any other type of promissory note. Even a personal check is, in its way, a substitute for cash; and so, of course, is a credit card.

Anthropologists remind us that there was a time when the medium of exchange in certain islands of the South Pacific was sea shells. Among American Indians it was wampum. In the Western states you could buy merchandise with an I.O.U. signed with an X. Historically speaking, then, once we abandon direct barter — say where a farmer can exchange two chickens and a bushel of potatoes for a bolt of cloth — we *must* resort to various artificial types of currencies as symbols of our willingness to pay for what we want.

When corporations create negotiable paper, they too are following this pattern. They are inventing a medium of exchange which meets their immediate needs.

Actually the corporations have no choice. There isn't enough cash in the United States to serve all the requirements of modern commerce. Credit — or debt — is the only solution. Its use increases every day. The total amount of America's public and private debt (as evidenced by bonds and other paper obligations) is now $1,267,000,000,000. Of this the corporations' share is about $446,000,000,000.

One can understand why, in September of 1966, the Federal Reserve Board became nervous over the possible effect of increasing such widespread indebtedness. Fearing the inflationary results of allowing credit to run wild, the F.R.B. tried to curtail bank loans. It argued that there had been a 20 percent annual rise in credit year after year — too much for economic safety. Possibly the Reserve Board was frightened most of all by the figure of $446,000,000,000 in corporate debts.

It *is* a frightening amount when you speak of it as debt. But paradoxically, it is not at all alarming — in fact, it is reassuring and even inspiring — when you change perspective and speak of it as a confident public's *investment* in private enterprise.

In 1956, while investigating various companies that could be acquired, Rik went to California. His old friend Haim Bernstein, having relinquished the career of a Hebrew teacher, had opened a gift shop in Beverly Hills. Visiting him, Rik urged Bernstein to come to New York and join the Rapid-American organization. "There are many things you can do," he said. "And I like to work with old friends." (Within a year Bernstein accepted the invitation.)

Also, Rik met Bernstein's sister. She was the secretary of Bernard Gerald Cantor, a partner in the Beverly Hills investment banking firm of Cantor, Fitzgerald and Company.

"Rik," she said, "you simply must meet my boss. You and he have so much in common!"

Rik agreed to stop next morning at the offices of Cantor, Fitzgerald. As far as he was concerned he was simply doing something to please Bernstein's sister.

But when he and Bernard Cantor shook hands they were sealing a lifetime business compact. They sat down and talked. Minutes stretched into hours. Rik's plans and vision excited Cantor. As an investment banker he recognized their possibilities. As for Rik, he was profoundly impressed by this financier's knowledge and acumen.

It was Cantor who flew to New York a few months later, in 1957, to urge Rik to buy control of the enormous company known as Butler Brothers.

This was an amazing proposal. Butler's sales amounted to almost $124,000,000 a year. One of its divisions was engaged in distributing merchandise to variety stores. Another owned five large department stores on the West Coast. In brief, this was truly a big league corporation.

(I asked Mr. Cantor to recall what had prompted him to approach Riklis of all people with this suggestion. There must have been scores of well-known financiers who would have been interested in acquiring Butler Brothers. Cantor mulled over the question. "I suppose the real answer," he said, "is that Rik had affected me as he had impressed so many others. When you talked with him you got a feeling of capability, of quiet common sense. And almost more important than anything else, you felt you could count on his being absolutely fair. As you probably know, he lives by the maxim that no deal is a good deal unless it benefits both parties. I knew he meant what he said.")

The background of Cantor's offer was this: A group of investors headed by Hans Dittisheim had previously bought a controlling interest in Butler Brothers. Bernard Cantor himself was a member of the group.

Serious differences of opinion had arisen between Dittisheim and his board of directors. As chairman, he disapproved of many plans for diversification proposed by the operational management of the company. Cantor was among those in disagreement with Hans Dittisheim. This dissident group, after long bickering with the chairman, finally decided to terminate the unhappy situation by placing control in other hands. Cantor, who owned approximately 10 per cent of the Butler stock, was offering Riklis the largest deal that had yet come to the young entrepreneur.

The investment banker told him, "You can buy control of Butler Brothers — 51 per cent of the stock — for about

$25,000,000. And there won't be any trouble acquiring the 51 per cent. A number of us are ready to go along with you."

Rik did not ask, "Why do you pick me?" He seemed to take it for granted that he was capable of handling such a deal. Instead he said, "Got the figures?"

From his attaché case — without which he never travels — Cantor produced Butler proxy statements and annual reports. Rik pored over them in silence.

He saw that Butler Brothers had over $8,000,000 in cash; $13,900,000 in receivables which could easily be turned into cash; another $15,000,000 in inventories. In other words, to buy 51 per cent of its stock for $25,000,000 would mean obtaining control of some $37,000,000 in quick assets.

Could it be done? By this time he had the millions that had been generated by selling several of American Colortype's plants. Moreover, Rik was negotiating the sale of the company's huge printing division (which, among other contracts, printed part of *Life* magazine). This sale would substantially augment his cash position and borrowing ability. With such Rapid-American assets behind him, Rik saw no insurmountable problem in raising enough cash to buy Butler.

When he had studied the statements he asked for a meeting with the dissident directors. He also requested a conference with the company's operating executives, A. O. Steffey and Emil Schram. "We must be sure of two things," he told Cantor. "First, will we be able to acquire full control of Butler Brothers, or will control be a matter of contention? Second, I want to look more deeply into the company's potentials."

Cantor agreed to arrange both meetings.

That evening, over dinner, Rik said to his wife, "Bernie

Cantor is in town. He wants me to buy control of a $124,000,-000 company. It means putting up about twenty-five million."

It was characteristic of Judy Riklis, of her complete faith in her husband, that she merely lifted her brows. "Are you going to do it?" she asked.

"If the terms can be worked out, certainly."

"You don't think it's too soon to take on anything so big?"

"I'm almost thirty-three. How long can I wait?"

In a matter of days Bernard Cantor arranged for the meetings Rik had requested, and Rik flew West. The first conference was with the Butler directors who were opposed to Mr. Dittisheim's policies. As they studied the unknown entrepreneur some of them must have had uncomfortable doubts. How could Bernard Cantor have picked anyone so young, so inexperienced in the affairs of a firm like Butler Brothers?

To counteract this, however, was their respect for Cantor himself. He was a level-headed, successful banker. He generally knew what he was doing and why. Besides, he had millions invested in Butler Brothers. He would hardly be staking his own interests on someone in whom he had no confidence.

The directors accepted Cantor's judgment. Rik was assured that his group could have a majority vote on the board — provided it acquired 200,000 shares of Butler stock.

Rik shook hands with them all.

A day later he met with Butler's operating management. They too agreed to go along with a new board. When he went back to New York the deal was settled in his mind. He would still have to convince his own directors that this was a good course to take, but when he called them into a meeting they promptly approved the idea — though its very size must have been staggering.

"So we proceeded to buy 200,000 shares of Butler stock," Rik later said, "and the Butler directors who had made this deal possible stood by their agreement. Our group was given a majority representation on Butler's board of directors.

"I must say that this launched three years of close association which I prized and enjoyed beyond all description. Butler's capable president, A. O. Steffey, and its equally able board chairman, Emil Schram, were dedicated men. We got along beautifully. This marriage of corporations, if you wish to call it that, lasted through three happy years.

"What eventually brought it to a close is another story. There was never any internal dissension. Rather, it was largely due to two facts: One was that, for a reason we were never able to discover, Chicago banks were wary of establishing a strong and lasting connection with the Butler company. Their lack of confidence may have been due to the previous dissensions in the Butler organization. Or else, maybe they felt they didn't know us, the new board, well enough. And secondly, we gave up Butler because, frankly, we faced what for us was a more attractive avenue of procedure."

But that happened later, after a period of extremely fast-paced activity. I say fast-paced because during the time that the Rapid-American Corporation held 51 per cent of Butler Brothers, it became engaged in a surprising number of other projects.

Among them was the acquisition of two midwest mail order firms, both rather small. But at this point in his career Rik had a purpose in buying even small companies. Each acquisition added to the total strength of Rapid-American. If this was to be his base of operations, it had to be sturdy. The bigger the base, the more respect — and credit — it would command in the financial community.

So he continued to study "special situations." He continued to seek companies which could be added to the Rapid-American complex. According to one of his associates, "Sometimes Rik reminded me of a juggler skillfully handling ten balls, all in the air, and thoroughly enjoying what he was doing."

I suppose all this could be construed as the road to success. But it must also be regarded as the road that led to difficulties. True, the difficulties were still some distance away, and nobody could foresee them.

For one thing, after the final merger of Rapid and American many changes occurred in the combination's structure. "The sale of our big printing division," Rik once explained, "had helped us raise the capital to acquire 51 per cent of Butler Brothers. But we still owned the other divisions of what had been American Colortype. One of these — producing Christmas cards, school supplies, gift-wrapping paper, and so on — operated under the name of American Paper Specialties. This eventually achieved annual sales of $20,000,000 with profits of about $1,000,000 before taxes. All was going well, and all of us worked like beavers."

But in spite of the efforts of the men around him Rik himself was working too hard, doing too much. One thing became clear: If the Rapid-American Corporation planned to acquire other companies in fairly quick succession, what it must develop — and develop at once — was a three-fold program. It needed, as Rik put it:

1. A team of experts who could "roll in and out of a specific situation," able to diagnose and solve its problems.

2. Training of Rapid-American's own personnel in broadened management procedures and techniques.

3. The creation of a reservoir of top executive talent — men who would be ready to work with new acquisitions of all kinds as mergers took place.

As for this last, top executive talent, Rik already had attorney Harry H. Wachtel as general counsel. Wachtel was later elected vice-chairman of the board. He also had Robert P. Miller (who had sold his Minneapolis advertising agency) as head of American Paper Specialties.

Wachtel's law firm had long used the services of two young partners in an accounting firm, Herbert Silver and Isidore Becker. They were both expert in tax problems. Because Rapid-American would need sound guidance in the intricacies of corporate taxes, Wachtel introduced Herbert Silver to Riklis.

Rik had met many accountants. A number of them had won his respect. But in the case of Herbert Silver he had an instant sense of empathy which none of the others had stirred. Silver and Rik were both quick, keen, instinctively attuned to the demands of high finance. As Silver's partner, Isidore Becker, said, "They clicked from the start. You know Rik. When he likes a man he immediately wants to work with him."

Herbert Silver not only became Rapid-American's chief accountant. He was soon elevated to the rank of financial vice-president. (He filled this position until his sudden death in 1963. Since then Isidore Becker has taken his place as financial vice-president. The executive officers of four large banks all have told me, "Becker has become the perfect complement for Riklis. He has one of the keenest financial minds in New York.")

Another executive Rik met through Harry Wachtel was the

head of two New York correspondence schools, Leonard C. Lane.

At the outset Lane was merely an investor in Rapid-American. Respecting Wachtel's judgment, he had bought a considerable block of Rapid-American stock. In fact, he had bought enough to entitle him to a seat on the board.

Rik wanted to meet this major stockholder. When he did their handclasp was accompanied by the kind of grin that comes to two men when they know they are going to like each other. Possibly this particular rapport was the attraction of opposites. Where Rik was short, swift, decisive, Leonard Lane was a big man — well over six feet tall, over two hundred pounds in weight—deliberate of manner, ingratiating, good-humored. Also, by coincidence, he was a suburban neighbor of Rik. Lane came into the organization as a board member.

Beyond cavil these were all able men who now surrounded Riklis. So were others who had joined him — Lorence Silverberg, Hal Divine, Haim Bernstein. They brought youth, energy, enthusiasm, and intelligence to the enterprise.

But none, it will be noted, had experience in retail merchandising, a circumstance which was destined later to expose Rik to serious criticism.

Still, as he himself summed up the first three years of Rapid-American's activities, "We did well financially by keeping our biggest investment, Butler Brothers, operating smoothly, well-protected, and its management happy; by generating cash and profits in Rapid-American, our parent company, while consolidating its activities; by building a strong management team for the present and for the future."

Curiously, it was during this period that Rik *almost* obtained control of what was one day to be his major acquisition — the McCrory-McLellan Stores. As early as 1957 he had learned from various bankers that the eminent financier, Roger Babson, was seeking a buyer for his holdings in United Stores Corporation, which controlled McCrory-McLellan.

Rik at once went to see Babson. He was not at all deterred by the fact that United Stores were doing an annual business of about $250,000,000; or that almost a half-century separated his generation from the industrialist's.

Rik's friends still smile at the visualization of that initial meeting. Babson, of course, was a man of mature years, mature experience, mature wisdom. Laden with honorary degrees, he had headed scores of business organizations, including his own Babson Institute. In 1940 he had run for the Presidency of the United States on the Prohibition Ticket. He was seventy-seven years old. In any single month he was quoted in the financial press as frequently as, say, Bernard Baruch. He was, in short, a giant among financial giants.

And what of the young man who sat on the other side of Babson's desk, earnestly offering to buy the immense McCrory-McLellan chain? Meshulam Riklis was still slight and boyish in appearance. He spoke with the Israeli accent he had never been able to lose. Babson must have been struck by the sheer nerve of this youngster who wanted to buy his securities. He had probably never before heard of Riklis.

The amazing thing is that the deal almost occurred. After a few conferences Roger Babson was about to agree.

But the venerable financier changed his mind. He had another offer from Bankers Securities in Philadelphia. It was this second proposal he decided to accept.

A year and a half later Bankers Securities resold the McCrory-McLellan stores to a man named Maurice Olen, an enterprising industrialist from Alabama who headed the H. L. Green variety stores.

And soon thereafter, in 1959, furor and dissension burst upon H. L. Green's board of directors. Auditors found discrepancies in the company's records. In a violent internal upheaval Maurice Olen's resignation was demanded and obtained.

Rik guessed the shaken H. L. Green board desperately needed to be rescued from confusion. This was one time when the steadying hand of new management might be welcomed.

He knew it would take close to $50,000,000 to buy and develop the McCrory-McLellan chain. But fifty million was, after all, a number, and Rik had never been deterred by numbers. He went off blithely to see the H. L. Green people.

As for the money he would need, it would have to be produced by the sale of Butler assets. In the annals of his rise, this was to be known as Operation Big Switch.

VII

A FEW evenings later, in talking with Mel Unterman on the telephone, Rik reported, "By the way, I was offered $45,000,000 for Butler Brothers today."

Unterman caught his breath. "By whom?"

"I don't know."

"What do you mean, you don't know?"

"I didn't ask. Arthur Anderson brought me the offer."

"And you didn't ask who was making it?" Unterman sounded stunned. "Rik, I can't believe it! Why didn't you ask?"

"Look, Mel, I want $50,000,000. Why should I care who offers less? I'm not interested. When Anderson comes up with a $50,000,000 offer, I *will* ask."

It was a typical and revealing answer. Rik has never had the patience for bargaining. He has never wasted time or even curiosity on pointless offers.

Within a few days, however, he was able to call investment banker Bernard Cantor to say the $50,000,000 price *had* been met. "I want to sell off every Butler division, every plant," he said. "The money we raise will come into the BTL Corporation. We keep the BTL Corporation. We sell only its assets." BTL was the New York Stock Exchange designation for Butler.

He did not have to detail the plan to Cantor. These two men spoke the same financial language. If Rapid-American were to sell Butler Brothers as a whole (of which it owned only 51 per cent) it would receive only 51 per cent of the proceeds — something more than $25,000,000. But if it sold only the *assets*, piece by piece, retaining the BTL Corporation to be the repository for all moneys received, it would through its 51 per cent BTL position *control all those proceeds*. And Rik preferred to control the disposition of $50,000,000 than to possess $25,000,000.

The proposal had come from the City Products Corporation. It was ready to meet the $50,000,000 price — $36,000,000 in immediate cash, the rest in notes.

The terms for this significant sale were arranged in November of 1959. The closing of the transaction, subject of course to stockholder approval, was scheduled for February of 1960.

It is not every day that an almost unknown businessman sells the assets of one corporation for $50,000,000 and immediately uses the money to buy an even larger company. Rik was suddenly catapulted into the financial columns of New York's newspapers. He held no press conferences, gave no private interviews. So writers had to speculate about him and his aims; but not for long. They grew tired of such speculation because other things were happening to fill newspaper columns: Khrushchev had just visited the United States and conferred with President Eisenhower; the first French nuclear test had just been exploded in the Sahara; seven countries — the Outer Seven — were forming the European Free Trade Association, an answer to the Common Market. In the face of such competition for public interest the negotiations for Butler soon dropped out of the news columns.

Everything went smoothly with Rik's plans. On the scheduled day in February, with stockholder approval obtained, the principals of the companies met in Chicago. By midafternoon, in a law office, all details were settled. Meshulam Riklis received a certified check for $36,000,000 and carefully put it into his wallet.

The negotiators left for the Ambassador East hotel to have cocktails. But at five o'clock Rik looked at his watch. "Gentlemen," he said, "if I leave now I can just catch the six o'clock flight to New York."

He shook hands with them all and departed. Downstairs he got into a cab. But then he remembered something. He jumped out of the taxi and rushed back to the group in the cocktail room. The first man he saw was Sid Luckman.

And now, with a $36,000,000 check in his pocket, Rik said, "Sid, can you lend me ten dollars? I don't have enough for the cab!"

2

There is only $40,000,000,000 of American currency in circulation. That is hardly enough to meet corporate debts of $446,000,000,000. What generally happens when securities become due is that they are replaced with new issues.

There is nothing alarming about such constant refinancing as long as corporations remain solvent and well managed. If ever American industry becomes shaky, however — if investors decide to demand their cash and hold it for a better time to invest — *then* America may face trouble. Just as we used to witness panicky runs on banks we could in such circumstances see panicky runs on corporations.

"But we don't have to worry about *that*," officials have said.

"Every government agency in the finance field is guarding against it."

Yet some people try occasionally to circumvent regulations, usually by issuing misleading information. In 1966 the economy observed a clear example of what can happen as the outcome of false financial reports. The Westec Corporation of Houston, Texas, had in a two-year period acquired fourteen corporations in such fields as mining, electronics, aerospace, and oil exploration. In buying these companies Westec had incurred paper-secured debts running into fantastic figures. It said it was anticipating profits of over $5,000,000 for six months. This projection plus the spectacular growth of the company had sent its stock zooming from $2 a share in 1964 to over $67 in 1966. Everybody was happy. When an investor's paper wealth is soaring to such heights, he never complains.

The thing that exploded Westec's position was a sober audit. This was so shockingly poor that creditors immediately demanded their money. At the same time shareholders sought to dispose of their holdings — and found no buyers. There was nothing Westec's management could do to escape a tidal wave of demands — nothing but to obtain more financing. Failing in this, they had to seek the refuge of Chapter 10 of the Federal Bankruptcy Laws.

The corporation's chief executive went to a hospital with a ruined stomach. The trustee appointed by the government studied the results of his first month's supervision and made the sad figures public:

Total revenue	$ 9,156
Operating costs	$200,821
Net loss	$191,665

Fortunately the American economy, strong and confident, is no more affected by an occasional Westec than Gibraltar is affected by a single wavelet. America must, however, regard Westec situations as warnings of what should be guarded against for the safety of shareholders.

On the stock market there certainly is no lack of confidence. An issue of corporate securities is often snatched up as fast as it appears. Indeed, the public's response to such issues sometimes seems so overwhelming (or absurd) as to be incredible. There was, as an instance some years ago, the case of the early dealings of James Joseph Ling.

James Ling incorporated as Ling Electric. His firm was so small that no financial company cared to handle its securities. So Ling set up a booth at the Texas State Fair; he also went from friend to friend with his offerings. The results of his personal sales campaign would probably make a professional financier writhe. The records show that in those days James Joseph Ling sold some 400,000 shares of Ling Electric, Incorporated, to the Texas public at $2.25 a share!

Happily for the purchasers, Ling proved to be an able and intelligent entrepreneur. He used the money to launch himself into making acquisitions and mergers. Today he heads Ling-Temco-Vought, Incorporated, selling $460,000,000 worth of electronic, aviation, and communication equipment per year. For diversification he has added the meat-packing Wilson and Company, an acquisition for which he borrowed $70,000,000 from some fifty sources, European and American, in early 1967.

He has built this complex of companies by the same method characteristic of most merger leaders; as one financial writer described it, "by a profusion of offerings and exchanges of virtually every type of security known to investors."

There is little point in speculating on whether such financing — a pyramiding of debt — is a healthy aspect of the American economy. It exists. It is as much a part of us as our language. So we must view the activities of all empire builders in the light of this reality.

3

The building of an industrial empire is not a process merely of adding acquisition to acquisition. Sometimes the basis of growth is *trading*. You sell what you do not need in order to raise the means of buying what you *do* want. You may sell plants, divisions, or entire corporations. As one man put it, "It's like building a successful ball team. Sometimes you have to trade players — even stars — in order to strengthen your position where it is weak."

Within ten days after disposing of the Butler Brothers assets Rik bought United Stores, which in turn controlled the McCrory-McLellan chain. (He also bought a 10 per cent interest in H. L. Green itself.)

There could be a serious drawback, Attorney Wachtel warned, in operating McCrory-McLellan through holding companies like BTL and United Stores: this was the danger of being classified as an investment company — which would subject the entire venture to different regulations.

In order to avoid this, and in order to be recognized as an operating company, BTL, United Stores, and McCrory-McLellan were merged into a single entity, the McCrory Corporation. This was accomplished through an exchange of securities involving no cash. Thus. BTL's $40,000,000 became available to the newly merged venture.

And now Meshulam Riklis, at thirty-six, found himself heading a chain of more than six hundred variety stores — one of the largest such chains in the United States — with total assets of over $70,500,000. His Rapid-American Corporation owned only 30 per cent of McCrory's stock, but this was sufficient to assure control.

One must remember that all this occurred in 1960 — hardly eight and a half years after he had begun to draw his circles in Minneapolis; hardly eight years after he had started as a $50-a-week junior analyst for Piper, Jaffray, and Hopwood. "This," his father said at the time, shaking an incredulous head, "can happen only in America!"

It was the beginning of one of the most active periods in Rik's career. As soon as brokers, bankers, and private agents realize a man is serious about making acquisitions, his desk is flooded with offers. Rik received them daily. Most were uninteresting. But there were others which not only intrigued him; he found some so right for his program of expansion, so perfectly attuned to his plans, that they became irresistible.

There was, for example, the Oklahoma Tire and Supply Company, with headquarters in Tulsa. Here was a chain of more than four hundred retail stores scattered over the Southwest. It was owned by a single family, the distinguished pioneer Sanditens of Oklahoma. They were asking $28,000,000 for their business. And they were showing earnings of $3,200,000 a year before taxes, $1,800,000 after taxes.

At first glance Rik might regretfully have put this opportunity aside. He did not think the company worth more than $24,000,000 (based on reasonable multiples of its earnings).

But when he studied its balance sheet more closely he discovered a way of agreeing to the $28,000,000 asked by the Sanditens, *yet buying Otasco for nothing!*

To put it more clearly, he saw a way of acquiring Otasco with its own funds, not using a cent of McCrory's money. Otasco had — besides $2,000,000 in cash — about $8,000,000 in accounts receivable.

"We evolved the plan," Rik explained, "of selling Otasco's accounts receivable and adding the proceeds to the cash Otasco had on hand. We could also sell some of their five scattered warehouses on a lease-back basis. This too would generate several million dollars in cash. So there would be at least $10,000,000 we could give to the Sanditens as a down payment, and the balance could be paid in equal installments over a ten-year period.

"Based on annual earnings of $3,200,000 before taxes, it was simple arithmetic to see that for ten years we could pay principal *and* interest out of those earnings — an average of a little over $2,250,000 a year — and still leave ourselves a profit. In this way we would ultimately come to own Otasco for nothing." That was precisely how it later worked out.

But meanwhile Rik struck an obstacle. Some of the Sanditens, a large family, objected to making the sale. They did not know him. One or two of the women who were shareholders thought of Meshulam Riklis as a New York slicker who was seeking some way to separate the family from its money.

This abrupt resistance caught Rik unprepared. He held a hasty conference with his accountant, Herbert Silver, and decided to fly to Tulsa. "You come along," he told Silver. "Maybe they'll feel better listening to a professional accountant."

In Tulsa he and Silver met first with Maurice Sanditen, the patriarch of the family. Sanditen was frank. "You're a stranger to us," he said. "Many of our people see no reason to turn the business over to somebody they don't know, somebody who may wreck everything we've built."

"As long as they feel that way I cannot ask them to make the deal," Rik agreed. "But before we make any such decisions I'd like to have the family know me. I want to know them, too. I'd like to invite them to dinner."

Maurice Sanditen smiled. "There are thirty-two of us."

"Fine. I want to meet them all."

Rik made arrangements for a private dining room at one of Tulsa's golf clubs. No doubt the members of the Sanditen family were prompted by curiosity as much as by financial considerations. Young and old, men and women, everybody with a shareholder's interest in Oklahoma Tire and Supply attended the dinner.

From the first course through dessert Rik did not attempt to talk business. He talked about a thousand other things. It happens that he has an inexhaustible repertory of wryly humorous stories, many of them emanating from his Hebraic background. Anyone who has pored over the pages of the Talmud knows that they are rich with anecdotes applicable to almost everything in contemporary life. Rik's Hebraic knowledge served him well that evening.

(And it has done so not only at the Sanditen dinner but on countless other occasions. Board members of the McCrory Corporation constantly speak of the tension and strain Rik has been able to ease with an apt Talmudic story. "He has so many of them," one man said, "that I sometimes suspect he makes them up. But who knows? And what difference does it make if the stories serve their purpose?")

The Sanditen dinner proved to be a relaxed, enjoyable affair. What Rik did at one end of the table Herbert Silver did at the other — between them, they established a friendly, uncomplicated atmosphere. Finally, when the meal ended, Rik leaned back in his chair and talked about the business.

"If this merger is approved by all of you," he said, "I don't expect any part of the present operation to change. *I* don't know anything about running Otasco; you do. So I'd hope that all of you who work in the company will continue. There will be no reduction in income for anyone. There will be no changes whatever except that you will become part of a nation-wide retail chain that will have over a thousand outlets."

He spoke and answered questions for almost two hours. Five years later, when I discussed all this with the Sanditens in Tulsa, they told me it was the most reassuring talk they had ever heard. "Rik became one of us. He made it clear that we all had the same common interest — good business for Otasco. As for us, apart from continuing to run the company and to lose nothing in income, we would be receiving cash and notes worth a total of $28,000,000, a sum we could get in no other way without paying enormous income taxes."

The circumstance which most pleased the Sanditens after a five-year association with the McCrory Corporation was this: "We have been allowed to run our business without interference. We never had the New York office looking over our shoulder, trying to tell us what to do. They have been wise enough to let us operate by our own know-how. We simply report to them twice a year. The result is that we are doing more business and showing more profits than ever in Otasco's history."

Has the entire family been content with the merger?

"Unanimously," Julius Sanditen said. "And we have a Sanditen on the McCrory board of directors."

Since Rik had sold Otasco's warehouses on a lease-back agreement to raise several millions in cash, I asked if this sale has caused any family resentment.

"Not at all," Sanditen replied. "Once you understood the deal, it made practical sense. And we're a practical family."

So Otasco became part of the Riklis empire. Into the parent company it brought new assets of approximately $19,000,000, annual sales in excess of $50,000,000. And all of this provided additional strength for further acquisitions.

VIII

THE Otasco merger marked the beginning of two years of swift growth; so swift, indeed, that one marvels at the number of mergers which were simultaneously being studied, discussed, and concluded.

Within a month after Otasco came into the organization it was followed by the National Shirt Shops. This was a chain selling boys' and men's furnishings. Again the method of payment was partly in cash, the balance by the issuance of convertible preferred stock. And again it really did not matter how much cash was expended. As Rik said, "It was immediately replenished by the excess cash held by National Shirt prior to the merger."

Since so many acquisitions were being negotiated at the same time, it is futile to be concerned about their chronological order. The major ones among them (as compared with the acquisition, say, of Economy Stores for less than $2,000,000) were undoubtedly the H. L. Green variety stores and then the famed Lerner Shops.

As for the former, McCrory already owned the 10 per cent of the Green chain which it had acquired while making the McCrory-McLellan purchase. Now Rik set out to buy more of the company's stock. H. L. Green would be a natural and profitable complement to McCrory-McLellan. And H. L. Green stockholders were receptive to offers.

No doubt one of Green's major attractions for Rik was its large Canadian subsidiary, Metropolitan Stores. This, he had ascertained, could be sold for a substantial sum. Also, H. L. Green owned a number of Olen stores; these too could be sold. With all such possibilities for generating cash to make the transaction appealing, Rik bought over 50 per cent of outstanding Green securities and thus turned McCrory-McLellan into MMG — McCrory-McLellan-Green.

This deal, like the others, involved payment in two ways: first, by the issuance of securities — convertible preferred stocks plus warrants; and second, by the outlay of some $22,000,000. In newspaper reports the $22,000,000 appeared to be an impressive cash expenditure. The truth is that it represented virtually no outlay at all. The quick sale of Green's Canadian holdings and of the Olen stores, as Rik had planned, at once brought back almost $22,000,000.

So once more he was able to cling to his principle of having acquisitions pay for themselves.

The widely publicized Lerner purchase presented a different kind of challenge. It had begun one afternoon in a discussion with several board members. Waving at the papers on his desk, Rik had said, "I've been going through a hundred suggestions for mergers. Not one measures up to the Lerner Shops as far as our needs are concerned."

What Lerner's had to offer was impressive. First, it had a distinguished reputation. It was one of the best-known chains of ladies' specialty shops in the nation. The affiliation would add incalculably to McCrory's image.

Second, it was prosperous. Its earnings were at that time exceeding $3,000,000 a year.

Third, it had excellent management. Harold Lane, Sr., and his son, Harold Lane, Jr., as well as Stanley H. Kunsberg, the operating heads, were recognized as leaders in merchandising efficiency. They would be an asset to any retailing organization.

Fourth, Lerner's had unlimited potentials for still further growth, and this was backed by its strong command of credit.

Fifth, Rik believed a controlling interest in the company could be bought for approximately fourteen times its earnings, or a total of over $40,000,000. This might be a bit high but not unreasonably so. The Lanes would have to be offered *some* management incentive among the reasons for joining the Mc-Crory complex.

One of Rik's associates, pacing the office with some nervousness because of the size of this deal, asked the obvious question: "Are Lerner's interested in merging?"

"I can't say," Rik admitted. "I've never discussed it with them."

"But has Harold Lane given anybody an indication of how he feels?"

"Can't tell you. I hardly know him. I've met his son now and then, but we didn't discuss business."

The men at Rik's desk glanced at one another and shook their heads. At this point the acquisition of Lerner's sounded like a pipe dream. The possibility seemed to exist nowhere except in Meshulam Riklis's mind.

"So what's the next step?" one man asked.

"I'll go put it to Harold Lane," Rik said.

Nobody has been able to analyze the self-confidence in Riklis — or is it pure nerve? — which enables him boldly to offer a stranger a price for something it has taken that stranger a lifetime to build. It was only a few mornings after this first conversation about Lerner's that he decided the time had come to see the head of the chain. This was in February of 1961. He was having breakfast with one of his associates, Jack Weinstein, when he said, "Let's go see Harold Lane."

Weinstein quite naturally asked, "Did you make an appointment?"

"No."

"Well, we'd better phone first."

"Too early. He won't be in yet." Rik rose from the breakfast table. "Come on. We'll get there about the same time he does."

He and a baffled Weinstein went to the Lerner headquarters. In a corridor they met Harold Lane, Jr.; and though he must have been startled by this unexpected visit, he readily arranged Rik's meeting with his father.

Some time later, when I questioned Harold Lane, Sr., about the unexpected call, he smiled. "I could guess what he wanted to talk about," he said. "He caught me at a relaxed time — after the Christmas reports were in — and I didn't mind listening. In fact, I was curious to know what sort of person he was."

(Here is a paradox. Harold Lane, Sr., had heard about Riklis. The heads of other corporations were familiar with his activities. So were bankers. But those elements of Wall Street responsible for giving a person his public image — financial writers, security analysts, customers' men — knew virtually nothing about him. Unlike other financiers, Rik had still held no press conferences, had sought no publicity. He was an enigma.)

"What particularly interested me," Harold Lane, Sr., said,

"was what kind of arguments he would present. I listened to him with attention."

Mr. Lane, almost thirty years older than his visitor, sat back in an attitude that seemed to say, "Show me." A man of powerful physique, with a deeply lined and craggy face, he could put a caller on his mettle merely by remaining silent, waiting, judging.

But Rik was prepared. What he said made the head of the Lerner chain thoughtful. Probably Rik knew that a man of Lane's wealth could not be swayed only by a substantial offer for his stock. But he also knew this: Harold Lane, Sr., was an extraordinarily able administrator. The success of the Lerner Shops was a reflection of his managerial skill. Nothing could appeal to his interest and imagination more powerfully than indications of how added efficiency could be brought to Lerner's management as well as to McCrory's.

Therefore the things Rik stressed were the arguments Lane later presented to his own stockholders when he sought their approval for the merger. They concerned administrative efficiency. Rik pointed out how a merger could achieve at least five goals. They are worth recording because they indicate the kind of thinking that appealed to someone who had not seriously considered a merger.

1. It could bring about large savings in administrative and overhead costs. Many of these would be absorbed into the operations of the joined companies.

2. McCrory's and Lerner's distribution expense would be cut by having the other members of the complex share in these expenditures. Thus, through consolidation of costs, the other members would be helping to increase profit ratios, and this in turn would benefit all stockholders.

3. Lerner's and McCory's unprofitable holdings (every chain has a few) could be eliminated without fear of letting able people lose their jobs. Placements could readily be found for them in other divisions of the parent empire.

4. Association with the McCrory Corporation and its affiliates would offer Lerner's personnel wider opportunities to rise to top levels of service.

5. Through the use of McCrory's widespread resources the Lerner Shops could find and develop new retail areas of their own.

These were some of the provocative possibilities Riklis brought into Harold Lane's office. It was the only approach which could conceivably have caught Harold Lane's interest. Whether it had been intuitive or carefully conceived, it served its purpose.

Actually, it *had* been logically thought out. If I stress this point, it is only to emphasize again the fact that every merger depends on reasons carefully considered before discussions begin; reasons which will appeal to the potential seller.

As for the five major points Riklis now made, in succeeding months they were the basis of many conferences; of staff meetings in both corporations; of problems and their solutions. Such preliminaries to the final Lerner acquisition consumed almost the entire year of 1961.

But when negotiations were at last concluded Meshulam Riklis had won not only a prestigious and prosperous addition to his empire, for which he had paid by an exchange of securities; he had also won in Harold Lane, Sr., Harold Lane, Jr., and Stanley Kunsberg three outstanding associates, three able board members, and three firm friends.

2

There was surprisingly little government interference in any of these acquisitions. For one thing, though many were horizontal mergers — that is, of companies in the same general business of retailing — nothing in these amalgamations either destroyed competition or restricted trade.

Rik was also leading the Rapid-American empire into the area of conglomerate mergers — those which combine wholly dissimilar companies. He bought Florida citrus groves from the Heller family; and he acquired the Cellu-Craft Company, manufacturers of plastic bags and allied products, from Samuel Levy and his partner, Sid Luckman, the ex-football star. Obviously the government had no reason to object to such diversification.

With each step he took in expanding his empire Meshulam Riklis himself underwent a subtle change. It was inevitable. He was gaining confidence and stature. He was proving that his original dream was not a gossamer thing. Now that he had demonstrated his ability, he could no longer be called brash when he approached other businessmen. His manner had to be described less condescendingly, and people spoke of him as "self-assured." The difference connoted the growth of the boy into the man, of the neophyte into the veteran.

Now that the Riklis family enjoyed the privileges of American citizenship — which entitled them to travel on American passports — they also had the other prerequisite for travel, a good income. They used their vacations to tour Europe and Israel.

On one trip to Tel Aviv, where he and Judy visited their many relatives, Rik discovered in dismay that his Herzlia High

School was being dismantled. On its site Israel was about to construct its first skyscraper, the Rassco Building, that would become "the tallest thing between Madrid and Tokyo."

The reconstruction of the Herzlia school on another location (as well as the building of dozens of additional schools) required a great deal of money. Much of this was being raised in the United States by the United Jewish Appeal.

Rik made a substantial contribution to the school fund — and his ability to do it gave him a new sense of responsibility. His money could be put to uses that would yield great dividends in satisfaction.

There was a rabbi who said to him, in appreciation of his gift to the Herzlia school, "I've often been told that Jews who go to America and become rich lose some of their religious zeal. Now you are making me believe that America and its wealth can *double* a man's zeal."

The rabbi was not wrong. When Rik came home to King's Point, Long Island, he gave many evenings to philanthropic demands as assiduously as he gave days to the demands of business. His home, in fact, became a gathering place for philanthropic conferences. He invited noted fund raisers for UJA and other causes to address groups in his living room. And it was at one of these gatherings that he asked Charles C. Bassine to speak.

Bassine, much older than Rik and president of Spartans Industries, had given a great deal of time and money to causes like the United Jewish Appeal. This evening he spoke with deep fervor to the guests Rik and Judy had assembled. When the meeting was over, Bassine lingered over coffee for a long talk. That first conversation — ranging over the problems of Israel, of Jews everywhere, and finally to the fascination of merging business to business — launched a friendship that became stronger with the years. It was a friendship destined one day to help lift Meshulam Riklis out of the bleakest despair.

3

The fact that in his business acquisitions Rik had no opposition from the government brings up a significant matter.

There are an astonishingly large number of federal agencies which have the power, through court action, to block mergers. Chief among them, of course, is the Antitrust Division of the Department of Justice. This primarily guards against the danger of any industrial combine becoming a monopoly.

But the Antitrust Division is only one watchdog of the merger trend. In addition one could name the Securities and Exchange Commission, the Federal Trade Commission, the Federal Communications Commission, the Internal Revenue Service, the Interstate Commerce Commission, the Federal Power Commission — indeed, almost any agency concerned with the welfare of the nation's economy. Nor can one omit the many state bureaus which are in a sense local counterparts of federal offices.

Individual stockholders too can and frequently do seek to stop their corporations from taking merger steps. When a corporation pays for an acquisition in stock, this additional block of securities thrown into the market can dilute the value of those already in shareholders' hands. "The more segments into which you cut a pie," says a Wall Street cliché, "the smaller each segment becomes." So stockholders at times have strenuously objected to such dilution of their holdings.

One shareholder who had protested the merger of two electronic firms (not in Rik's organization) told me: "I'm seventy-four years old. I invested in this company because I felt its dividends would contribute to my income at an age when I *needed* such income. I'm not interested in a merger which will bring bigger profits to other people in a few years. I need the money *now*. If there's cash to be spent, distribute it in dividends!"

Also, in any merger there is always the danger of unfavorable union reaction. Some entrepreneurs have tried to buy a controlling interest in a competing company merely to liquidate its assets for quick cash, at the same time eliminating a competitor. Or else they bought plants with the idea of moving them to other regions where labor or tax conditions were more favorable.

Such tactics could conceivably deprive a community of many jobs. They could create a ghost town. So it is understandable that unions and civic officials have occasionally fought to prevent an acquisition from being consummated on the grounds that it could destroy the local economy.

Obviously, then, the thousands of mergers that materialize without challenge do so for the simple reason that the benefits they promise outweigh all other considerations.

But this must be said of government attempts to block mergers: *Do they not infringe on that aspect of free enterprise which entitles a person to buy or sell his property as he pleases and to whom he pleases?* Has the government the right to interfere with such freedom of choice?

A nice problem. Legal minds have not yet settled it to everyone's satisfaction.

4

I was once present at the initial discussion between two men who were contemplating a partnership. One had begun to list his assets when the other interrupted: "Never mind what you've *got*. The question is *how much can you borrow?*"

Bank credits have become invaluable in an age that so frequently demands large-size financing. And the larger the company, the more it usually needs to borrow.

Rik's need for *cash* has always existed. Not every corporate transaction can be made with the issuance of securities. For one thing, labor cannot be bought that way. When a complex of companies like Rik's employs between 60,000 and 65,000 people, it has to meet its enormous payrolls with cash. It must also pay cash to the manufacturers who supply goods for some 1,500 retail outlets; these men have their own payrolls to meet.

It is true that retailing may produce heavy flows of cash, especially when more than 1,500 stores pour their receipts into a common pool. But this flow can be erratic. It depends too often on seasons, on weather, on competitors, on similar variables. It does not guarantee cash the instant it is required. Credit is always essential.

It is a remarkable commentary on the enterprise Riklis was building to note that even in those early days the banks which were supporting Rapid-American were such venerable institutions as The First National of Boston, Chemical Bank New York Trust, and Franklin National. One might also note that Rapid-American enjoyed the benefit of sizable loans (in the millions) from both the Massachusetts Mutual Life Insurance Company and the sternly conservative, rigidly cautious Ford Foundation.

How had he won the support of these institutions? The first time I put the question to Rik he merely shrugged. "You get loans where you apply," he said. "Nobody ever got a cent where he was *afraid* to apply."

To put it simply, he had as little timidity or hesitation in approaching a bank as he had in approaching the prospective seller of a business. The worst that could happen would be a refusal. And that was not likely. He made no unreasonable requests. With a few successful transactions behind him, he had already established the kind of character bankers respected; he had proved his ability to repay all debts. At the age of thirty-eight he was heading an empire with net assets of $66,000,000 and sales of almost $600,000,000 a year.

He had another advantage, too. All of the businesses he had acquired had, before coming into his organization, enjoyed credit lines of their own. They had long-standing associations with many banks. And so each new acquisition gave Rik access to new banking resources. Everything considered, he was pleased.

"We had a good combination of diversified companies," he said, "and a strong management team. Employees' benefits had been raised to standards almost unheard-of in the past. We wanted to make them all conscious of their membership in one 'family.' "

This was 1962, and the stock market was beginning to slip. But it was not yet slipping for Rapid-American, whose shares had risen to sell at $37 — a record high.

Curiously, the press was giving only sporadic attention to the affairs of Meshulam Riklis. *Fortune* magazine had printed the first of its articles about his rise — an extremely laudatory piece by Irwin Ross — and his various acquisitions had been duly noted in New York's newspapers.

As for his non-business life, he was discovering the obligations of success more sharply than ever. Philanthropy was, one might say, being thrust upon him. He was now receiving requests from a veritable plethora of Jewish institutions — colleges, seminaries, hospitals, synagogues, organizations like B'nai B'rith, many more.

This must be said: he responded with a generosity that few had anticipated. From the start he made a practice of setting aside 20 per cent of his personal income, sometimes 30 per cent, for these donations; and he shared the American credo that corporations themselves have obligations to support their community projects.

The gifts he gave brought him many new friends. Rik found himself being invited to spearhead campaigns, to serve on charitable committees, to sit on boards of trustees. On these he worked with some of the most distinguished Jewish philanthropists in America. Albert List, Charles C. Bassine, Sol Kittay — the list was long and brilliant. Being the youngest among them, Rik came to be looked upon as a promising Jewish leader of the future.

Outside of the philanthropic world he joined another group — the businessmen in the Young Presidents' Organization. This is composed of men who achieved company presidencies before the age of forty. And whereas in philanthropy Rik met with the older generation, here in the Young Presidents' Organization he met men of his own age.

He was happy in both circles.

But in spite of this contentment there was — paradoxically enough — something about his business that he found unsatisfactory. He called it "an internal situation that has to be remedied."

The many divisions of the McCrory empire were, for the

most part, being efficiently run. Lerner's was doing better than ever. So, under continued Sanditen management, were the Otasco stores. National Shirt Shops also were operating well. This vast enterprise, however, needed one thing: an experienced executive who could coordinate all operations and raise the entire company to even higher profit levels.

The McCrory Corporation, through its McCrory-McLellan-Green stores and through the Lerner, Otasco, and National Shirt chains, was oriented principally toward retail merchandising. Rik's own talents admittedly lay in the realm of finance. He felt he had to find an experienced man who could coordinate the merchandising operations of the empire. For such an expert he launched a nationwide search until he found the man he wanted and his assistants.

The new group plunged into its duties with spectacular plans. One of these, an innovation, would be the establishment of "McCrory Villages" in Tuscaloosa, Alabama, and Stillwater, Oklahoma. These were to be the first of a series of huge shopping centers. Each McCrory Village, as envisioned, would bring together in a single setting the McCrory-McLellan-Green stores, the Lerner Shops, the National Shirt Shops, and every other facet of the McCrory complex which would logically fit into such a venture.

Another innovation was the equipment of "Shopmobiles" — modern variety stores built into automobile trailers. Like mobile libraries, and also like the itinerant peddlers of another era, the Shopmobiles were designed to carry McCrory-Mc-Lellan-Green goods to communities which lacked such stores. (It was an imaginative plan, but it never worked well. Perhaps people distrusted an itinerant merchant. To whom could they turn if goods proved unsatisfactory? What kind of guaranty could you expect from a retailer who would be gone by morning? Perhaps, too, they enjoyed credit in their local shops; you could hardly ask credit from a trailer-truck which might not visit your community again for many months.)

Nevertheless, McCrory's seemed vigorous. "Our enthusiasm was at an all-time high," Rik said, "when the stock market took its setback in mid-1962."

Practically all stocks slid downhill. McCrory's, too, suffered a drop. Yet Rik was not dismayed by the recession. Confident that a strong corporation must recoup minor losses, he surprised his fellow board members by calling the situation a blessing in disguise. Up to this point Rapid-American had owned only 37 per cent of McCrory's stock. Now that its price had dropped, Rik saw the general market slump as an opportunity to buy more shares of McCrory at low cost and achieve a 51 per cent indisputable ownership.

"My thinking was prompted," he explained, "by the feeling that we would probably never again be able to buy McCrory stock so reasonably."

The board agreed. But it would require some $15,000,000 to buy the number of shares necessary to increase Rapid-American's holdings to 51 per cent. This meant borrowing more cash from banks — cash which would be secured by those McCrory securities already in Rapid-American's possession.

The buying program proceeded well. (By the time it was completed, Rapid-American had $44,000,000 invested in its cornerstone company. And its control of McCrory was incontestable.)

But trouble was now on the way.

Throughout these months of strengthening the McCrory holdings Rik had left operational duties to the new management team. He himself was studying the many merger opportunities constantly coming his way. (People and firms who arrange such deals receive high finders' fees; $100,000 or more is not an unusual sum for bringing two firms together. Some investment bankers have earned millions for initiating a single merger. So there were many offers.)

Rik spent busy months on prospective acquisitions and on the financial aspects of the companies involved. If sales at McCrory's were not quite matching earlier projections of earnings, this could be attributed to the recession that was affecting the entire nation. Few people were worried. The American economy was resilient. It would snap back to normal.

Meanwhile he performed his own task of strengthening Rapid-American's position in McCrory.

In addition he had begun to explore the possibilities of an affiliation with the great Glen Alden Corporation, headed by financier Albert A. List; and he had been casting tentative glances toward Charles Bassine's Spartans Industries. But there was nothing conclusive about these possibilities.

In the late months of 1962, with everything apparently under control, Rik felt he had earned a vacation. He and his wife left for a European trip with the Young Presidents' Organization.

He had no idea of what was to happen until, dressing one evening in a Vienna hotel, he received a telephone call from Bernard Cantor in New York.

"Rik," Cantor said, "I advise you to catch a plane and come home. We may be in for trouble."

About to fly to Moscow with the Young Presidents' group, Rik was hardly prepared for this kind of interruption. He wanted to know what had happened.

"*Barron's* magazine," Cantor told him, "carries a very unfavorable story about you and McCrory's. I think you'd better come back. In fact, we all think you'd better come back."

When Rik put down the telephone he stood staring at the wall while Judy watched in perplexity. A strange thought went through his mind. Was it wise for a corporation head to be out of the country at a time when his company came under some sort of attack, even a mild attack?

And also, would a man like Cantor be advising a return unless he considered it urgent?

Rik turned to find Judy watching him in silence. "We've got to go home," he said.

She studied his tight face. Then she nodded and turned away. "You take care of the tickets," she said. "I'll pack."

IX

LESS than twenty-four hours after receiving the telephone call in Vienna, Meshulam Riklis walked into his offices at 711 Fifth Avenue in New York. He was tired after the unexpected flight, but he certainly did not look frightened. If anything, he was resentful.

"What kind of organization have we got here," he demanded, "if the president can't take a short vacation without being called back? Why all this panic over a magazine article?"

("I believe," one director said to me long afterward, "that he had deliberately planned to meet us with that kind of reprimand. By showing his own lack of concern he probably hoped to make us all feel easier. As in an army, a leader must never show fear.")

Cantor, Miller, Wachtel and others had summoned all available board members for a conference. They were waiting for Rik and they looked disturbed.

"Let's see the article," he said.

He read it in a silent conference room. A dozen men watched him across the long table, seeking to fathom his reactions from every nuance of expression in his travel-weary face.

The article bore the title, "Meshulam Riklis Is Trying to

Build a Retail Empire in a Hurry." It was written by Lawrence H. Armour, a name strange to Rik.

The piece began with a few disarming lines. It marveled at the fact that while most retailers' stocks had dropped sharply — including those of giants like Sears, Roebuck — McCrory's had held up surprisingly well. This sounded like a compliment.

Then the article's tone abruptly changed, a caress becoming a slap. It said the McCrory stock was selling "at infinite multiples of present earnings" in spite of "lackluster" management and poor sales records.

The writer sought to explain the unreasonably high price of McCrory's securities by quoting stock exchange statistics. These indicated that Rapid-American had recently added 44,200 shares of McCrory to its holdings; it now owned 41 per cent of McCrory securities and intended to continue to buy until it achieved 51 per cent. The inference was that the company's large purchases of its own securities explained the abnormally high price level they maintained.

To finance this program, the author reported, Rapid-American was offering $2,300,000 in new debentures.

In 1957, the article went on, the McCrory Corporation had been capitalized at only 2,300,000 shares. This number had been consistently augmented so that there were now 5,500,000 shares outstanding.

"If McCrory's makes money," the *Barron's* article predicted, "it will take a long time to filter down to its stockholders."

And stockholders faced even further dilution, the author warned, because of more options, warrants, and convertible preferred stock being issued, "representing 4,600,000 additional shares."

At this point Meshulam Riklis stopped reading to look around the table at his silent board of directors. On the infrequent occasions when he becomes angry, he is capable of flinging out a word or two of quiet, pithy profanity in any of three languages — English, Hebrew, or Yiddish. The directors expected to hear all three. Instead Rik spoke calmly. "Are you scared by all this?" he asked. Nobody answered. If ever there was a real collapse of McCrory stock they were all in danger of losing millions. The company's securities had already, in the past few months, followed the stock market trend by going down. Confronted by silence, Riklis said nothing else. He went on reading.

The article now suggested that "knowledgeable stockholders had sold their own shares at a favorable price," a procedure "smacking of impropriety."

It made one visualize insiders on the board, with some secret knowledge, dumping their securities; or else, selling them at a profit to Rapid-American while still sitting on Rapid-American's board. This latter course, if true, would have put directors in the untenable position of using the funds of other stockholders for the purchase of their own shares.

As a matter of history, this was not true. Yet several stockholders eventually did come to believe it. They brought conflict-of-interest suits. In a way the suits were fortunate since they served in the end to exonerate those charged with the malpractice. One director had indeed sold 2,500 shares — that was all — while the corporation was buying 1,500,000.

As for the director who had sold those 2,500 shares, a considerable portion of his holdings, he later told me that he had been obliged to meet a bank debt of his own. "I had to let go of what I owned or I'd have gone bankrupt," he said.

"Selling was not a matter of trying to make a quick buck. Nor did it indicate any lack of faith in McCrory. I simply had no choice. Yet the *Barron's* article made me look venal."

But on this day in October of 1962, as Rik sat with his directors, the action of one particular board member was not the principal matter at issue. Rik insisted that McCrory securities offered a sound investment at their present low price. The company was strong. It would yield good earnings.

As every board member knew, annual figures in retailing depend largely on the *second* half of the year — the half including back-to-school and Christmas sales. For this period prognostications were excellent.

"It is ridiculous for us to panic on account of this article," Rik said. "As far as I can see, there is nothing to be done about it today, anyway." He looked at his watch and rose from the table. "Gentlemen, I've flown in from Vienna, and I'm tired. I want to get some sleep. I don't think there is any ground for worry. The meeting is adjourned."

2

Long after that article appeared — in fact, several years later — I asked Rik how he had really felt on reading it. Had it jarred him as it had evidently shaken some of his directors?

"No," he said. "I thought they were making a mountain out of nothing. The article was inaccurate because nobody from the magazine had studied our records. I'd gladly have shown them. They might have given the writer a true picture of our operations. But *Barron's* was privileged to print its opinions, right or wrong, and I wasn't too disturbed."

"You had no misgivings about McCrory's future?"

"Absolutely not. Why should I? The company was strong. I had complete confidence in it."

"How about the directors?"

"They were all confident. Do you think we would have continued buying more and more McCrory stock if we didn't believe we were making a sound investment?"

"And yet the stock eventually went way down."

"Yes, but not because of the *Barron's* article. That did not produce a crisis. I won't pretend I liked what it said or even its tone, but what happened later had no connection whatever with that magazine piece."

The volatile, super-sensitive reactions of the American stock market to any event, great or small, are often puzzling beyond explanation. One would think that seasoned financiers, being in general men and women of substance, are hardly the most insecure of people. One pictures big investors as solid citizens — "the real owners of the United States," as some of them call themselves — with minds that are clear, practical, strongly intrenched in their convictions. They are the bulldogs of society. They are unshakable.

But is this really so?

I have often suspected that nobody has less faith in his own judgment than the American investor who "plays the market." I have seen him spend hours of every day either on the telephone with his broker or studying the actions of the Big Board. The slightest sign of change leaves him sweating and anxious, not sure of whether to buy or sell or do nothing. A day or two earlier he may have bought a security with the greatest confidence. That confidence can vanish as swiftly as it rose. One man whom I watched during his Florida vacation spent more time on the telephone talking to his New York broker than on the golf course or in the swimming pool. He would have done much better by vacationing in his broker's office.

What troubles the typical investor? Everything. A paragraph in a financial column may merely ask a question, but if the query even *suggests* weakness in a corporation it can prompt many to sell their holdings. Vague rumors and misinterpretations have caused as many fluctuations on Wall Street as any solid reason one can pinpoint.

Both the American Stock Exchange and the New York Stock Exchange try to combat the effect of false rumors by keeping stock-watch procedures constantly on the alert. Any abnormal fluctuation in a security's price is promptly investigated by the exchanges' surveillance divisions. If it proves to be based on rumor, the corporation involved is asked for a clarifying statement. In this way harmful rumors are often crushed before they can do much damage.

But there are some occurrences whose results nobody can control. The effect of a single national event or a single presidential statement can be either calamitous or stimulating, and nobody can predict which it may be.

An excellent illustration of this occurred when President Johnson made his State of the Union address in January of 1967. At 9:30 that evening he asked Congress to approve a 6 per cent surcharge on corporate and private income taxes. The next morning stock market prices collapsed. By noon the trend had been reversed, and prices were soaring. No doubt this midday change occurred in some measure because millions of buyers sought to take advantage of the sudden low prices. But whatever the cause, those prices rushed upward to finish the day with a tremendous gain. The New York Stock Exchange recorded the third largest daily volume in its history — a total of over 13,000,000 shares changing hands. They had gone down and come up again *because of the same Presidential words!*

When I asked various bankers and stockbrokers for their opinions as to what had caused over 13,000,000 shares to be bought and sold in a single day, I had so many varying answers that they constituted no acceptable answer at all — except perhaps that the financial market is allergic to *every* form of pollen.

Of course, the article on Rik in *Barron's* magazine did precipitate rumors and uncertainties. Why had the publication printed this particular story? I discussed this with the editors long after its appearance.

Riklis, they said, was a pioneer. Having successfully shown how empires could be built without starting from a productive base, he now had many imitators. And many were pyramiding debt to proportions which *Barron's* saw as a peril to the nation. Riklis himself might lead investors to success, but other entrepreneurs could easily lead them to disaster.

In an effort to comment on the growing merger phenomenon — an effort to light a danger signal, as it were, for all investors to see — the magazine analyzed what it viewed as the outstanding merger program of that particular time. It chose Riklis's empire as the example because it had grown to such amazing proportions. *Barron's* intention, according to its editors, was not to depreciate McCrory's stock, thereby undermining the company's investors. Rather, it was attempting to call attention to the possible dangers inherent in the swift building of *any* huge industrial complex whose structure rested on a foundation of debt. It saw Meshulam Riklis's achievement merely as a symbol of what was beginning to happen throughout the country.

Shortly after the *Barron's* piece appeared, a strange assault was made on the Riklis empire. It was ugly, subversive, and hidden behind a mask of anonymity. Somebody — his identity has never been learned — prepared a spurious five-page analysis of Rapid-American and McCrory. The statistics were inaccurate. The conclusions were as astonishing as they were wrong. This so-termed "balance sheet" indicated that McCrory's could not escape collapse. This communication was mailed to McCrory directors in an unmarked envelope giving no clue of its sender.

A day or two later another anonymous envelope brought the same people copies of the *Barron's* article.

The purpose? As Isidore Becker, the corporation's Financial Vice-President, has pointed out, "Somebody was evidently trying to depress our stock. He must have known that we were buying all the shares we could obtain in our efforts to get 51 per cent of McCrory's. Quite a few people were selling McCrory's short — it was a perfect setup for short selling. They were selling to us at current prices, gambling that the stock would go still lower, when they could buy it. Whoever the anonymous letter-writer might be, he was obviously trying to depress our stock."

The effect of this sudden wave of anti-Riklis activity made itself felt.

Since a retail chain cannot operate without adequate credit, it was the fear of seeing this credit diminished that worried McCrory's directors.

There were two obvious courses to take. First, Rik could — indeed, he must — sell off some of Rapid-American's less profitable assets. This could generate cash. Second, he could seek a merger with a strong group whose assets would help weather a possible crisis.

During the past year Rik had already reinforced Rapid-American's cash position by disposing of the mail-order firms he had acquired. They had been a drain, and he had not regretted letting them go.

Rik wasted no time in bemoaning these necessary steps. As he pointed out to his directors, the elimination of loss operations like the mail-order firms might actually be a healthy thing. The important consideration now was to maintain the soundness of the McCrory company. On this foundation, as Rik saw it, everything else must be built.

He pursued his second plan, too: to seek a new merger which would strengthen Rapid-American's position.

With this in view he visited several business leaders. One was Charles Bassine of Spartans Industries, Inc. Bassine, an eminently successful industrialist, had already engineered a number of mergers of his own which had forged a strong business complex. Listening to Riklis, he was clearly interested.

But being a shrewd and prudent man, Bassine deferred any decision until he could study McCrory's full sales report for 1962. This would not be available until early in 1963. Until then he decided to postpone further discussion.

That merger never occurred.

For the definitive McCrory earning figures were issued in April of 1963. And they brought a shock.

Part Three

◆

THE YEAR OF ORDEAL

X

A CORPORATION which shows a year's profits of $3,000,000 would normally be regarded as fairly successful. Those were the approximate 1962 earnings of the McCrory stores. What reduced the figure to disquieting proportions was the fact that McCrory's management had projected substantially higher earnings.

The difference troubled the banks.

Their worried officers hurriedly met at the Commodore Hotel in New York. There were men from the Chemical Bank New York Trust Company, the First National Bank of Boston, The Franklin National Bank of Long Island, the First Western Bank and Trust Company, the First Nevada Company, as well as representatives of the Ford Foundation, the Massachusetts Mutual Life Insurance Company, and others, including investment banker Bernard Cantor. In addition to the money due to them Rapid-American owed some $13,500,000 on the convertible debentures it had issued as a further means of acquiring 51 per cent of the McCrory stock.

And now *Barron's* published a second story — this time an editorial which in effect said, "We warned you."

Newspaper columnists too leaped into action. Here was a subject that was dramatic, fresh, contemporary. A financial columnist might argue that he owed it to his readers to supply them with "inside" information which could affect their future investment decisions.

The cumulative result of such publicity, however, was to turn Meshulam Riklis and his corporate activities into a *cause célèbre*. One writer, Leslie Gould of the *Journal American,* devoted a long series of columns to McCrory and Rapid-American.

Until that moment nobody had ever tried to compare Riklis with the unsavory manipulators who had flashed across the financial skies in the past only to explode and bring ruin to those who had followed them. The Kreugers, the Gutermas, the Ponzis, the Gilberts, men of that breed had always been a class unto themselves. The secrecy and deception with which they operated were bound to lead to their downfall. By contrast the Riklis ventures had all been conducted openly, with the knowledge of every government agency that cared to study each merger; with the awareness and approval of stockholders. What was unfortunate — perhaps even questionable in its ethics and taste — was the tendency of some financial writers to ask rhetorical questions like: Is Riklis Another Ponzi? Is McCrory's About to Crash?

Merely to pose such questions is to plant doubts in investors' minds. Anyone who took the trouble to read the answers supplied by the same writers might well conclude that the Riklis saga *was* different, that he was *not* pulling strings behind a wall of secrecy. The trouble was, of course, that people often concentrated on the queries, not on the answers; just as readers accept the implications of newspaper headlines without bothering to study the details.

The center of the storm, if one can call it that, quite naturally was Riklis himself and his board of directors. The board's meetings suddenly became harsh and noisy and confused. Some of the directors, adopting the language of surgeons, insisted that when gangrene sets in you must amputate at once before it spreads to destroy the entire body.

In this case, "gangrene" referred to the new team of executives who had been hired to manage McCrory's. They had projected greater earnings than they had produced. Such an error could not be tolerated. It was believed to be the basis of all this present trouble, and there was only one way of responding to its mistakes.

The entire team was summarily dismissed.

As for the bankers, they were becoming more alarmed than ever. Seeing McCrory's securities continue their downhill slide, they had good reason to worry about their loans to the company. Also, they were becoming angry.

What they needed was a whipping boy. It is futile to be angry unless there is someone to be angry *at*. The only one around to fill that unenviable position was the leader of the enterprise, Meshulam Riklis, who had solicited the loans.

Overnight the financial genius of one day became the financial villain of another. A few of the bankers began to mutter that the first intelligent thing to do must be *to get rid of Riklis*.

If this action was not immediately taken it was because Rik had a few staunch friends among the bankers. There was Bernard Cantor, who never lost faith in him; there was Don Miller of the First National Bank of Boston; and there were others like Pat Clifford and William Renchard. They asked who would take Rik's place if he were ousted, and nobody had an answer.

"I couldn't altogether blame them," Rik has said. "They had

seen us dismiss our top management — an amazing move. Added to this they now discovered that our cash position, so strong in the past, had deteriorated because of the disappointing earnings. To make matters even worse, we had a very high inventory on our hands and costly fixed plant expenditures."

Nor was the confusion limited to banking circles. Manufacturers too were frightened. McCrory's owed *them* money. And stockholders were alarmed, even panicked, as they saw their shares go down and down.

A few resorted to legal action. Not that their suits were later sustained, for no illegalities had occurred. But Riklis and other directors found themselves beleaguered by more than a dozen legal challenges.

Worst of all, perhaps, was the turmoil that continued in the board of directors itself. One's instinct, when things go wrong, is to blame the other fellow. Rik, naturally, was "the other fellow." He was not, however, the only target of tirades.

Harry Wachtel, lawyer and vice-chairman, found fingers pointing at him, too. Why had legal counsel permitted this thing to occur? What was more, by what right was a lawyer serving as vice-chairman of a corporation devoted to retailing? What could he possibly *know* about retailing? He was an attorney, not a businessman. Some of his colleagues informed him that the best thing he could do would be to resign as vice-chairman. The resignation would at least show creditors that Rapid-American was trying to set its own house in order.

Wachtel quietly resigned the vice-chairmanship. The board elected businessman Leonard Lane to take his place.

Bernard Cantor of Los Angeles has for years maintained a New York apartment and a New York office at the Regency Hotel on Park Avenue. As an investment banker Cantor has in his time witnessed many a business crisis but nothing quite like this.

"How to clear up the mess was a problem for which nobody had an answer," he said. "Night after night a group of us would meet at my apartment, trying to find a way out. It was the only time in our long association that I ever saw Rik look beaten and unsure of himself. I remember wondering sometimes how it must feel to rise to great heights in a few short years, only to be dumped back like this — suddenly, unexpectedly, into a maelstrom of debt and anguish, wondering if he had lost the credit and the confidence of bankers."

Rik himself said, "The absolute shock I felt in those days is something hard to describe. For a while I must have acted like a zombie. My condition, my foggy state of mind, seemed to penetrate to every corner of our company, to every part of its management. We were all dazed."

The bankers fared no better. They met again and again. One of them broached the idea that Harold Lane, Sr. — the eminently successful head of the Lerner stores and himself a director of the Riklis empire — be urged to become board chairman of the McCrory company. Maybe an able businessman of his type could still change this operation into something that could ultimately show good earnings.

When the bankers asked Lane to take the post, he refused. He could not and would not elbow Riklis aside. By this time the two men were staunch friends. Lane would not jeopardize that friendship. "If there is anybody who can get McCrory out of this predicament," he assured the bankers, "it's Rik himself."

The bankers turned to another industrial leader, Albert List of the Glen Alden Corporation.

List too rejected the offer. Like Harold Lane, he had come to know and admire Rik; but this was not his only reason for scotching the idea. List was in his sixties. He was an immensely successful man, wealthy, devoted to philanthropy and to the collection of art. He simply had no desire, at his age, to become a troubleshooter for the bankers. Besides, he too felt that Rik was the logical person to lead McCrory's out of its troubles.

So the bankers were stymied.

2

This was the worst period in Rik's life. It lasted many weeks. At home Judy, his wife, found it hard to recognize her strained, worried husband. Where was the relaxed, humorous Rik who had always found so much delight in his King's Point home, in his children, in family ties?

All sense of pleasure and relaxation was gone. He spent most of his time at his office or at Cantor's office with lawyers and financial advisers. When he came home he looked physically and emotionally drained. It was during these desperate weeks that Riklis developed the ulcer with which he has since had to live.

In normal times the board of directors would meet approximately once a month. Their main purpose had been to hear Rik's progress reports. With everything going well nobody had bothered to oppose a leader under whose management Rapid's stock had climbed to $37 a share.

Now, with shares down to $4, there were constant meetings. Nervous directors were always pacing the offices and the corridors at 711 Fifth Avenue. Whenever two or three of them got together, there were conferences, arguments, whisperings.

Rik was drawn into many of the discussions, but for the first time in his life he became a silent listener.

In these dark days he wrote a moving letter to his father in Israel. Long ago he had advised the elder Riklis to invest what he could in Rapid-American and McCrory. Now he wanted his father to know what was happening. "But I want you to know," Rik added, "that I myself do not intend to sell a single one of my shares. I know that McCrory is a sound company. Some day the value of its securities will return."

Pinhas Riklis promptly wrote back: "No, I will not let go of my shares. It is not so much that I believe in McCrory as that I believe in you. I beg of you not to lose courage. Your mother and I know that you will come through this difficult time, and in a way this adversity may prove to be a blessing for you. For you will learn many things from it. You will come out a much stronger man."

The elder Riklis did not limit himself to giving advice. Knowing that their son needed all the moral and emotional support he could find, Rik's father and mother at once flew to the United States. Except for occasional brief visits to their homeland, they have remained in New York ever since.

Those of his associates who were closest to Riklis during the long period of trial — men like Harry Wachtel, Haim Bernstein, Leonard Lane, Isidore Becker, Robert Miller, Hal Divine, Bernard Cantor and a few others — all concurred on one point: adversity served to reveal the real man.

He had a profound sense of responsibility to those who had trusted to his leadership by following him into this critical situation. He knew that the biggest McCrory and Rapid-American investors were not necessarily people who could afford the loss they were sustaining. A few board members had borrowed every possible dollar on their McCrory securities in order to buy more McCrory stock. This might have been a fine exhibition of faith in the company's future; or it might have been faith in leverage. But was it wise? With Rapid's stock now down in the $4 area, Rik feared that some of his friends might be wiped out.

He talked to each of them in private. Were they in need of funds? If so, he offered to share what he had, or to borrow in their behalf, or to sign notes for them.

"You don't forget offers like that," one of them told me. "To me it disclosed the Riklis behind the financial facade — a Riklis who was a far cry from the ruthless, hard-driving tycoon some columnists were picturing. A few men needed help and took the money he offered. I myself did not. But I did clasp his hand in appreciation. From that moment I knew we'd be friends for life."

If Rik gave friendship, he received it too. As I have indicated, he had been active in Jewish philanthropies ever since coming to New York. Most of the gifts had gone to causes like the United Jewish Appeal, the Jewish Theological Seminary, Brandeis University. He had attended philanthropic meetings where he had come to know intimately some of the men he had encountered only briefly in business.

And now, at the depths of his misfortunes, these friends came to his aid. Charles Bassine of Spartans Industries, Sol Kittay of the BVD Corporation, Eli Black of the A. M. K. Corporation, Albert List of Glen Alden — their astounding confidence in this young financier was demonstrated by the generous help, encouragement, and support they offered. If Rik accepted assistance it was to help those of his own friends who were in serious straits.

(To each of these men who stood by him he later sent a letter of gratitude. One of them said to me, "I shall always treasure that letter. It was a vindication of everything I believed of the man.")

It has often been said that nothing reveals loyalty as much as adversity. Rik found it true not only among his friends but in his immediate family. And there it manifested itself in deeply moving ways.

His wife, Judy, offered to close the King's Point house, move into a small apartment, and find a job. She intended to resume the first work she had done in America — teach Hebrew. Work and adversity were no novelties for Judy Riklis. A *sabra* — a native born Palestinian — she had been reared in a sun-baked land inured to struggle. Though her family, the Sterns of Tel Aviv, had been of the upper class in both their economic and cultural status, every one of them had had to work hard; every one knew the perils of living in a country beset by constant danger. A sabra, the native fruit of the Holy Land, is rough and tough on the outside, soft and sweet on the inside. If ever Judy had indeed been tough on the outside, her years in America had changed her outwardly so that no visible sign of toughness remained. But now, as she declared her intention of going to work, much of the old hardihood suddenly reappeared.

Rik refused to listen to such plans. Yet she insisted. And then, unexpectedly, their daughter Simona stunned them and settled the issue.

She walked into the room to interrupt the discussion. At eighteen Mona was ready for college. "I've decided to put off school for a year," she announced. "I'll get a job."

Both Judy and Rik were deeply touched, but the family's

dedication to learning had come down through generations of scholars. The one thing they could not permit was a postponement of college. They had to show Mona that things were not *that* critical. It was this abrupt need which drained away Judy's resolution to change her way of life. She had to prove to her daughter that, despite all adversity and setbacks, the father of the family was still capable of caring for his own.

So Rik's plea to his wife prevailed. Judy continued to run the King's Point house on as modest a scale as she could; and Mona was persuaded to go to college.

Much later, when Rik himself came to speak of those trying months during which nobody could foretell the rigors of the future, he allowed himself only a phrase or two about his own emotional condition. He said:

"It took a long time before I was finally able to concentrate, able to sift through problems, to separate and evaluate the dilemmas we were facing. But one day my mind seemed to snap clear. I was able to cope with each problem separately. How to save the company?

"The question of money came first. The value of our Mc-Crory stock investment was down from $55,000,000 to $28,000,000. Short-term debt was heavy and pressing. Part of our long-term debt was fast approaching default unless it could be extended and modified. Could we meet these payments?

"In the case of McCrory our worst problems lay in the danger of a credit squeeze, particularly with back-to-school and Christmas business coming soon. The inability to buy goods in time and at proper prices might permanently damage the company.

"And too, the variety division of McCrory-McLellan-Green

was demoralized in the matter of personnel. Remember that the entire cadre of top executives had been dismissed. Inventories were high. Losses were mounting. And there was no leadership.

"There were other problems, too, not the least of which were the several stockholder suits. But they were not as immediate as the others. So I concentrated on trying to solve the important ones first.

"What to do about Rapid-American seemed obvious. Everything it owned must be liquidated to meet our obligations and to leave us still owning 51 per cent of McCrory. The future of Rapid, I was convinced, must be tied stronger than ever to the fortunes of McCrory.

"Despite the poor showing the McCrory stores had made in 1962, I insisted this could one day be a great and profitable chain. It had all the potentials."

Studying the 1962 records in detail, he could see which stores had lost money, which were laden with unsold inventory. He could almost point to those with efficient management, to those with bad management. And he began to formulate a plan.

The significant thing, of course, was that Riklis was recovering from the initial blow of the April report. Like a boxer who suffers a punch that leaves him stumbling and groping, he now shook his head, blinked, and threw off the stupor. He was again thinking clearly.

"You could see the old Rik coming to life," one of his assistants said. "It brought a feeling of courage into the office. For a while, anyhow. Until he got the worst blow of all."

That happened the day the bankers sent a committee of one to see him. He began by assuring Rik of the high regard the banking community had for him personally. But they had been reviewing the McCrory situation detail by detail.

First, McCrory's was undoubtedly the victim of costly management deficiencies. Second, nobody could avoid facing the unpleasant truth that Riklis himself, heading a chain of retail stores, knew little about retailing. Third, though the Riklis method of financing the purchase of 51 per cent of McCrory's stock was entirely legitimate, it could lead to a loss of public confidence.

There were other things the bankers' representative had to say, many of them. He assured Riklis that he had supporters in their ranks. In fact, he acknowledged that several of the men were ready to trust in his ability to extricate McCrory's from its predicament. But "several" did not constitute a majority. And the majority, having for weeks been patient, had now come to a definite conclusion.

"Rik," the banker said, "the group wants you to resign."

Meshulam Riklis did not immediately reply. He turned to gaze at a window.

He was pale and drawn. Mechanically he took from his pocket one of the pills he had of late been swallowing to ease the pain of his ulcer. His fingers played with it, then put it back. In those silent moments Rik sent his thoughts over ten years of planning, dreaming, struggling. It was as if, in a single tableau, he could view everything that had happened since he left the employ of Piper, Jaffray, and Hopwood.

If he quit now, he realized he would forever be known as the man who had led an empire to catastrophic failure. At forty, he would be finished. What investor, what bank, would ever again have reason to trust his word? All the magnificent dreams, all the ambitious charts he had constructed out of circles, all the pioneering ingenuity for which he had once been applauded — all this and infinitely more, including his self-respect and the well-being of his family, the welfare of the friends who had supported him — all these would be irretrievably lost.

He drew a deep breath and turned back to face the banker. "No," he said, "I will not resign."

"But Rik, you have no *choice*."

"You're right. I have no choice at all. I have to stick. It's you bankers who have a choice."

This puzzled the visitor.

Rik said, "You can, of course, choose to throw me out. You have the power and the votes. And then you can throw the whole McCrory operation into bankruptcy. That will cost you millions. It will cost our stockholders more millions. That's *one* choice."

He paused to let the possibility have its effect.

"Or," he went on, "you can give me the time to lead McCrory out of this chaos. Nobody knows the present setup better than I do. Nobody has studied it as I have. I know exactly what has to be done. I want to lop off all losing operations. To raise cash, I want to sell off every Rapid-American asset *except* the McCrory chain. I am confident that I can make McCrory's a strong, profitable enterprise. And if you men give me the time to do it — if you will give me an extension of credit to see me through this period — there is no reason why any of you should lose a single penny."

He spoke quietly, with his old confidence. He told the banker how much cash he intended to generate by selling Rapid-American's assets. He outlined what he planned to do with the McCrory stores. When he finished he said simply, "The choice is yours."

The banker considered in silence. After a time he said, "This is something I'll have to take up with the others."

Rik nodded. "Let me know."

They rose. They shook hands. Before the banker went out he glanced back. Rik was seated again, still pale. He was staring at the window like a man seeing deep into the future.

A few days later the telephone call came. "Rik," asked Don Miller of the First National Bank of Boston, "do you think you can show any real results by the end of the year — say in eight months?"

"I think I can, yes."

"Good. We've decided to go along with you."

XI

THE respite granted by the bankers became, for Rik, a period of drama. It was now clear to him that there can be serious danger in acquiring businesses without being thoroughly cognizant of their operations. Conversely, it was also clear that good businessmen, applying good business principles, must be able to cope even with unfamiliar situations. They must prove the validity of the theory called "transference of ability."

Rik began by summoning his vice-chairman, Leonard Lane, and the newly appointed vice-president of Rapid-American, Samuel Neaman. The latter had come into the organization with a remarkable background of international experience. Rik had first met Neaman twenty years earlier when he was driving a chaplain's jeep in the wake of the British Eighth Army. Neaman was a major then — a Palestinian like Rik who had joined the British forces. The two men had frequently had long talks within sound of gunfire.

Even in those days Rik had admired Neaman's quiet, pragmatic intelligence. In ensuing years they had corresponded, and Rik had known that his friend had become a management expert. He had worked for various European firms. Later he became general manager of Consolidada, a steel producer in

Mexico, where he acquired so sound a business reputation that Rik offered him an executive post in the Rapid-American empire. He was to be general manager of the retail stores.

At the beginning, when Neaman came to join the organization, a few directors were dubious. Another non-retailer in a retail organization?

"No, I'm not a retailer," Neaman conceded to the board. "But I know business. And retailing *is* business."

Any doubt board members may have had about him were soon dispelled. At board meetings Neaman proved himself, in his quiet way, to be efficient and full of wise counsel.

"I'm here only temporarily," he informed his staff when he became general manager. "Until things get straightened out." Before long, however, he — whose advent had once caused a few heads to shake — was regarded as one of Rik's most inspired discoveries.

Both men, Neaman and Lane, agreed that the Meshulam Riklis they confronted now, in emergency conference, was a new kind of personality: determined, intense, staccato of speech.

"There must be reasons," he said in that new clipped tone, "that will show why these stores turned in only $3,000,000 in earnings. We've got to find what those reasons are and correct them. And we've got to do it *fast*."

It was evident that he had a plan. Lane and Neaman waited, not interrupting.

"The three of us," Rik announced, "are going to cover every store we can reach in the next month. And I mean by personal visits. We're going to study their operations. We're going to find out what's wrong. The store managers and district managers may be able to tell us a few things. But above all I want new ideas. The old ones haven't worked."

Not even an hour was lost. Neaman and Lane hurried home at once to pack. So did Rik. And the research trips started the very next morning.

For several days Rik and Leonard Lane traveled together. In this way they were able to use the first stores they inspected as guinea pigs; they were able to agree on general areas that had to be studied in all stores. What was the physical appearance of a place? What was the ratio of sales space to storage space? How much dead inventory was being carried? Why? How was the manager meeting local competition? What were his complaints, his explanations for unsatisfactory sales?

Samuel Neaman was doing the same kind of research in the areas he covered. Rik and Lane worked eighteen and even twenty hours a day.

"In order to save the daylight hours for the stores," Lane said, "we traveled from town to town at night. It was a grueling life. We covered about forty towns. Then we parted and went our separate ways so that we could double the number of places we visited."

The thoroughness of the research can be measured by the fact that the stores visited by Rik, Lane, and Samuel Neaman totaled over 500! They covered almost every state.

Among the things that became evident was that many managers required greater autonomy. No one in New York could dictate precisely how every store in every other state could best serve its own community. New York could operate *buying* offices; but local branches must indicate what they could sell, and these special needs must be satisfied.

Another shortcoming that became apparent was the antiquated condition of many stores. If they were to compete with modern establishments they had to be refurbished. Moreover, the vast inventories they had accumulated would have to be disposed of for whatever cash they could bring. Live dollars were better than dead merchandise.

All this was but the start of McCrory's Operation Bootstrap. When the research trips were completed the three men — Rik, Lane, and Neaman — gathered in New York to compare notes.

There were numerous reforms necessary on which they all agreed. But how were these to be put into effect in hundreds of stores? And how could anyone be certain that changes beneficial to one store would be equally helpful to others?

"We'll test," Rik said.

They selected an outlet in McCrory's District 5 — Long Island — to serve as the first model. Into this they poured all the ideas they had gathered from their five hundred case studies. They supplied fresh merchandise, got rid of the old. They changed everything from lights to window displays. They denuded storage space of goods which had never moved. They ran exciting advertisements in local newspapers.

Rik, Lane, and Neaman personally remained on the premises to see what would happen. The store manager, who had never before seen even one of the corporation's executives, must have felt that a new day had indeed dawned.

Almost overnight the model store in District 5 doubled and almost tripled its sales. People probably came to it in curiosity. They wanted to *see* the changes the advertisements had described. And the store continued to do well.

Rik then summoned the manager of the other seventeen branches in District 5. They spent days studying the factors that had stimulated business in the "showcase" outlet. Then they were directed to install those same changes in their own stores. "You will have all the backing you need," Rik assured them.

In a matter of weeks District 5 was reinvigorated. It became apparent that its total business would be tremendously increased.

With District 5 showing such success, the district managers of other areas — sometimes of entire states — were brought to Long Island to see what had been done and what *could* be done. Sam Neaman was now in complete charge of the reform movement. He ordered every district manager to set up a demonstration outlet in his own area, based on District 5; then he could spread the changes to the rest of the region's stores.

"This has to be a radiating procedure," he declared. "We want what happened in District 5 to be duplicated throughout the country. If there are branches that cannot respond, we'll have to close them. We just can't afford to hang on to losers."

To stimulate the cooperation of managers the company announced a new incentive program. McCrory's would pay generous bonuses predicated on the kind of increase that had been set by District 5. And now, everywhere in the United States, the slogan of McCrory employees became "To be alive beat District Five!"

There were still those who said (and probably will always say) that though Meshulam Riklis might have extraordinary financial genius he knew nothing about retailing. But the recovery he engineered for the McCrory stores in 1963 resulted in profits so high that at the end of the year the managers shared over $1,000,000 in bonus money!

Merchandising experts began to view Riklis in a new way.

Sol Cantor, one of America's leading retail merchants, the president of the great Interstate Department Stores chain, once told me, "If what Rik demonstrated was ignorance of merchandising, all I can say is I'd like that kind of ignorance working in my behalf!"

"The most significant thing about it all," said the vice-chairman, Leonard Lane, "was the birth of fresh spirit, of fresh enthusiasm, throughout our entire organization. You could feel it. You could hear it in the way managers talked. From the day we walked into their places and came to grips with their local problems they seemed to know that a new day had come for everybody. We were all determined to make the operation succeed. When you get that conviction shared by everybody, nothing can stop you."

Once he had launched the means of helping local managers, once he saw stores operating with new vigor, Rik turned to supervising the second part of his program: to raise cash by selling off Rapid-American divisions.

"After we've made McCrory a solid base of operations," he told his board of directors, "we can resume our expansion program. But right now, to achieve a firm base, we've got to liquidate everything we can to generate cash and reestablish our credit."

This in itself revealed the change which McCrory's crisis had brought about in his thinking. In earlier years Rik had been opposed to liquidating the major, well-paying divisions of any acquisition he might make. "We cannot afford to get the reputation of destroying that which we buy," he had often said. "That kind of reputation will make future acquisitions impossible. People have to understand that we plan to develop and build the firms we acquire."

But the catastrophe that threatened forced him, at least temporarily, to abandon such a posture. The directors never disputed the argument that the primary concern must be to regain borrowing capacity, and the only way to do it was by drastic measures.

In his determination to convert a number of holdings to cash, Rik had sold the Florida citrus groves back to the Hellers. He had sold the Cellu-Craft company back to Sid Luckman and Samuel Levy. In fact, he now sold almost every former acquisition except the Oklahoma Tire and Supply Company and the Lerner Shops.

As a matter of record, in order to improve McCrory's position he *tried* to sell Lerner's. "It would have been a heartbreaking thing to do," he admitted. "But I wanted to show the bankers that we were ready to make any sacrifice in order to meet our obligations. We had actually gone so far as to entertain an offer for Lerner's from the Glen Alden Corporation."

The proposed sale of Lerner's, however, brought quick stockholder opposition. Lerner's was doing more business than at any time in its history. McCrory stockholders protested that it was folly to separate McCrory's from a division which was generating rich profits. The plan to sell was defeated by vote (a decision in which Rapid-American did not vote its own 2,600,000 shares; it preferred to respect the wishes of the other stockholders).

Even without the Lerner sale the bankers must have been impressed. All figures indicated that a miracle was being achieved. Within less than six months McCrory's had generated almost $30,000,000 in cash!

The revival of trade throughout the McCrory-McLellan-Green stores was truly inspiring. It was now evident that at the pace they were setting the outlets would show a healthy earning improvement for the year.

But one man did not share in the excitement. It was during this tense, hard-driving period that Herbert Silver, the first Financial Vice-President of McCrory's, died.

For Rik the tragedy was stunning. He lost a close friend and an able assistant. But he instantly asked Isidore Becker, Silver's partner who had become Financial Vice-President of Rapid-American, to take Silver's place. Since that day Becker has filled it with what bankers have called "fiscal brilliance."

McCrory's recovery continued. Slowly, slowly, as reports spread, the value of the company's securities rose from its $10 low. And the rise was like a gauge of Riklis's spirits. They rose too.

There was a day when his daughter Mona returned from the University of Michigan for her Christmas vacation. That evening the entire family gathered around the dinner table—Rik and Judy and their three children, Mona, Marcia, Ira. The talk centered on Mona's studies. Suddenly she looked at her parents with eyes that were extraordinarily bright.

"I'm so glad you made me go to school when I wanted to quit last year," she said.

Judy assured her daughter, "There was no reason to quit."

"But Daddy seemed so — beaten."

At that Meshulam Riklis put down his knife and fork. He gave his daughter a hard look. "I may have seemed tired," he said, "but not *beaten*. No man is ever beaten till he gives up. Did you hear me give up?"

"No," Mona admitted.

"So don't ever say I looked beaten."

Was he oversensitive about this? Only Judy knew. She said gently, "Your father never talks about being beaten. It's just that when things go wrong he sometimes finds it hard to smile."

2

Every gardener knows that if you prune dead branches off a tree you cause the living branches to flourish more abundantly than ever. This is precisely what happened to McCrory during the final months of 1963 and in 1964. It lopped off some fifty dead branches—those stores that were sapping the life-blood of the chain with their losses.

Meanwhile Sam Neaman gave his attention to the surviving outlets. He provided their managers with everything they required, from new fixtures to new merchandise — and the bankers studied earnings reports intently.

At the home offices in New York and at the company's distribution center in York, Pennsylvania, all buying was now geared to the needs the local managers expressed. The latest electronic methods of tabulating inventory were installed, the latest automatic equipment for controlling general administrative expenses.

By early 1964 it became apparent that a miracle of rehabilitation was being achieved.

By September, in making a semiannual report to shareholders, Rik was able to announce: "All divisions are operating profitably. Second-quarter earnings this year advanced to $1,355,000 on sales of $129,171,000, compared to earnings of $620,000 on sales of $125,347,000 for the second quarter of 1963.

"The profit improvement resulted from the dramatic prog-ress at the McCrory-McLellan-Green Variety Division (MMG) coupled with profit increases at the Lerner Shops Division and the Otasco-Economy Stores Division. This was the first time since 1960 that the Variety Division achieved a first-half profit. Here are some highlights of operations:

"Store inventories are $8,000,000 below the same period in 1963. Sales incentive and cost control programs are operating effectively. The activities of the York, Pennsylvania Distribu-tion Center (McCrory's main storehouse) have contributed both to cost reduction and distribution efficiency. Shipments from the Center this year are *four times that of the first six months* of last year. All stores of the Division are now being serviced by the Center."

Shareholders welcomed the news. Those who had clung to their holdings throughout the depressed months saw their judgment vindicated. (Financial writers who had cast shad-ows over McCrory's future only a few months earlier now remained silent.)

Rik's half-year report concluded with the simple statement: "We are greatly encouraged by results and expect continued progress for the remainder of the year."

The banks were delighted. These were the days when the bankers would come into the Rapid-American offices just to tell Rik, "You're doing better than any of us dared expect."

Rik said, "What we need now is the assurance that we will have all the credit we require for further improvement *when we need it.* A revolving credit line would do."

The bankers met again. This time they consulted in a spirit of optimism. The losses they had dreaded no longer threatened them. It was evident that with proper support McCrory could be one of the country's best credit risks.

So, only a few months after he undertook to revitalize the chain, Rik received what he had requested from a syndicate of banks. It was a credit line of $57,000,000, more than he had ever had before.

Describing those days, Rik said: "It was almost miraculous the way everyone responded to the tasks at hand. It seemed that the will of all was to prove that the pulse-beat of this vast company was strong and healthy.

"Lerner's and Otasco, too, produced new records in sales and profits. It was as if they were trying to show that they could be counted on completely in this crusade for recovery."

Yet all was not well.

The lingering trouble was that the confidence regained by the banking community was not yet shared by the investing public. Wall Street — security analysts, financial writers, brokerage houses — still remembered 1963. For them the image of the McCrory Corporation, like the image of Meshulam Riklis himself, was still clouded by some of the uncertainties of the dark days.

At a meeting of McCrory directors one of them said, "What do we *do* about improving the company image?"

Another declared, "We need a high-powered public relations program. A campaign that will make the McCrory name shine."

Rik shook his head to all suggestions for a publicity campaign. "You can't buy a permanent good image with publicity alone," he maintained. "The only thing that will give us a better image is continued growth, stability, balance sheets that show steady gains. Those three have to go hand in hand —

with steady growth as the number one requisite. The publicity will come later. As we grow they'll *have* to write about us."

He aimed at achieving growth in two immediate ways: to expand the McCrory-McLellan-Green chain by opening new stores in good locations; and to resume a program of acquisitions which would broaden and enrich Rapid-American's status as well as McCrory's.

"This time we need a truly outstanding acquisition," he said at the board meeting. "One so big, so dignified, so strong that it will prove to the public that coming to live with us is regarded as a privilege by the most respected corporations in the land."

There was a moment of expectant silence. Then one of the directors asked, "What company do you have in mind, Rik?"

He answered, "Glen Alden."

Sooner or later one fact must become evident. Just as Glen Alden was chosen for the prestige and strength it would add to McCrory, as well as to its earnings, so every acquisition since the formation of the Rapid-American Corporation had its purpose. Unlike the early choices of Balcrank, Smith-Corona, Gruen, and so on, the later firms were not picked merely because they were available. Some — like Cellu-Craft and the citrus groves — were acquired to lend capital strength to Rapid-American itself; others, like Otasco and Lerner's, were bought to increase the stature and business of McCrory. None was a haphazard selection. Each was sought because it would logically fill a need.

And this, for the past ten years, has been the philosophy that has animated the growth of the Riklis empire: each acquisition or merger must be prompted by *a reason*. No company is bought simply because it can be had.

There are entrepreneurs, however, who buy everything in sight for no perceptible reason except to become bigger and bigger. And there are groups of corporate management who apparently fear loss of control to the big purchasers of their stock. These people are buying other companies as a *protective* measure. They want to become so big that they will be beyond the reach — indeed, beyond the interest — of those who might normally buy them.

As an example, the New York *Times* reported in May of 1967 that: "The Glidden Company, in a fight to block a bid for control by the Greatamerica Corporation, reached an agreement in principle yesterday to merge with the SCM Corporation. The proposed transaction involves stock valued at $251,125,000." And other corporations, too — fearing the result of someone's tender offer to their stockholders — have sought refuge in expanding to proportions (to use the British phrase) "beyond an easy take-over."

It is a game with many facets, this thing called empire building by merger. Though pioneers like Riklis may have constructed their corporate edifices with sound motivation, it is becoming evident that some followers have more devious purposes. One can only hope that their activities will not invite further government regulation.

Though I respect the need for a certain amount of such regulation — every area of society must observe sensible rules — I abhor the thought of *too much* government intervention. This can be stifling. It can convert government from being a public servant to becoming a dictator.

But the danger of having a few reckless entrepreneurs indulge in merger practices that are of a dubious nature must inevitably invite closer government scrutiny. Mergers which are not in the public interest or at least beneficial to stockholders can be a threat to American business. We ought to recognize this before it is too late; before Congressional committees set out to devise new controls. The best way to thwart the danger is to have business turn away from merger offers that make no sense.

Part Four

THE YEARS OF
NEW DIMENSIONS

XII

A GOOD many businessmen who like to play golf during the week justify this by assuring everyone that they do business on the golf course as well as in their offices. I do not doubt that in many cases this is true. It is significant only because it leads to a broader truth.

If the Riklis saga can be taken as an example, many origins of transactions — merger or otherwise — can be traced to social, community, philanthropic, recreational and other outside-the-office activities. Parkinson may not have incorporated this fact in his Law, but the more successful a man becomes in business, the more demands he encounters that draw him *away* from business. The president of an insurance company finds himself giving hours every day to raising endowment funds for his university; the head of a motion picture company leads a drive to build a new hospital; industrialists are drawn into all kinds of praiseworthy but totally extracurricular activities. And it is a good thing — an inspiring aspect of American life and social responsibility.

The effect of outside activities on a man's thinking often has a direct bearing on the way he conducts his business. "Every man I meet outside the office teaches me something," Rik has said. "Many of them have led me to new opportunities."

169

This broadening of interest is of course a salutary thing not only for the man himself but for his corporation. Years ago, in Minneapolis, Rik had to concentrate wholly on the personal problem of building an investment syndicate; there was little time for anything else, and nobody tried to divert his energies from this pursuit.

But as his strength and influence increased in New York, he faced the same demands that come to most industrialists. And this phase of a merger-making career would be inadequately recorded if it did not take into account the new dimensions of interests — indeed of personality — that come with affluence.

If Rik had not given a generous amount of time and money to demands outside of business he would surely have missed some of the warmest and most valuable friendships of his life — and I include his association with the head of the Glen Alden Corporation, Albert A. List.

Few American financiers have had a more distinguished career than List's. At the time Riklis first spoke of merging with Glen Alden, Mr. List was noted not only as a businessman but as a philanthropist and a collector of art. The grounds of his Connecticut estate were filled with sculpture for which any museum would happily pay millions. His home was an art gallery that reflected a remarkable taste in modern paintings.

But beyond all this, Albert List ("Abe" List to his close friends) represented solidly organized American wealth. His Glen Alden Corporation was itself the result of many acquisitions. A leader in the textile industry, it also owned the RKO theaters and Blue Coal. It was a major factor in leather tanning, among other areas. For Riklis to acquire such an equity would instantly raise his empire to the upper strata of American business.

To quote Leonard Lane, "It took guts even to *suggest* approaching a company like that."

To Rik it was not a matter of courage. This was a deal that made sense. He had studied the Glen Alden situation thoroughly. He knew that he could offer no less than $25,000,000 among other considerations. But he also knew, as he informed his board, that the purchase "would command the use of *at least* $25,000,000 now in Glen Alden's banks and twice that amount after certain liquidations and a period of cash generation."

But would Albert List be interested in a merger?

Rik's friendship with the financier convinced him that the head of Glen Alden had certain desires in life which he would very much like to fulfill. Now in his middle sixties, he would find deep gratification in devoting himself more actively to his many philanthropic interests. He would enjoy time to make a more concentrated search for art. Perhaps above all else he would like to know that the Glen Alden Corporation would continue always to provide security for those who had assisted in its growth. And he had no son of his own to carry out such an assignment. This last point, however, had to be balanced against the fact that he had a very capable nephew, Austin List, in the business.

Nevertheless, in every man's life there comes a time to consider retirement — or at least to give more time to the enjoyment of those rewards for which he has worked. It was possible that Albert List had reached that stage.

There was another factor involved, too. As it was later revealed in a proxy statement: "Glen Alden is involved in a number of present and potential court and administrative proceedings related to past and present coal operations. Some involve, or may involve, alleged air pollution claimed to be attributable to burning culm (refuse) banks. In a case brought by the Commonwealth arising out of these charges a decision *favorable to Glen Alden* was sustained by the Supreme Court of the State of Pennsylvania on the Commonwealth's appeal to that court."

Other court actions of a similar nature were pending, but as the proxy statement added, "Management has continued to maintain reserves for all such liabilities which in its opinion are adequate to cover amounts which Glen Alden may be required to pay."

Judged by precedents, then, Glen Alden's legal position was sound. It had already been absolved in one pollution suit and would no doubt be absolved in others. The significant question was: Would not Albert List be relieved, at this stage of his career, to let someone else assume responsibility for defending these court actions? They were undoubtedly millstones about his neck, even though some might be classified as nuisance cases.

With all this in mind Rik drove to List's home one weekend to discuss a merger. They sat on a lawn overlooking Long Island Sound and they talked.

Albert List once told me, "If there was *anyone* with whom I would have considered merging, it was this man. I liked him. He had intelligence and integrity, and I admired the way he had come out of his 1963 troubles. Anybody who could survive that ordeal could handle any kind of crisis."

Talking to List, Rik was frank about his plans for Glen Alden's future. The least profitable holdings were the coal company and the leather tanning division. If a merger were concluded he intended to dispose of these. As for the RKO theaters, though their receipts had shrunk, they could in his opinion be rehabilitated and brought back to high earnings. This was a task he expected to place in the efficient hands of Leonard C. Lane.

To all this Albert List gave throughtful attention. He was not a man to commit himself, his life's work, and his future on impulse. But when he shook Rik's hand in farewell that day both men were fairly certain that their affiliation would become a reality.

The meetings of lawyers, accountants, bankers, and others consumed many months. List himself readily agreed to make his personal holdings available for the deal. The question was, would other Glen Alden stockholders support the move? Would they offer their stock to the Riklis group, or had the 1963 problems of the McCrory Corporation left a sense of uneasiness among investors? No one would know until the result of a tender offer revealed how shareholders really felt about joining the McCrory empire.

The tender offer was duly made with the blessing of the bankers. Rik and his board waited to see what would happen.

What happened was that 800,000 shares of Glen Alden stock, in addition to Albert List's, poured in to consummate the deal. These people "took their profit and ran." But 75 per cent of the stockholders refused to sell their shares. They preferred to remain with the new management.

It was as gratifying an endorsement of McCrory's new stature as one could ask. In October of 1964 McCrory found itself owning 49.7 per cent of Glen Alden's common shares. It had won not only prestige but combined cash resources of almost $70,000,000.

2

What, then, was Rik's position in early 1965? As the creator and operating head of Rapid-American he directed that corporation's destinies. Because Rapid-American owned 51 per cent of McCrory's, Rik thereby controlled McCrory too. And now McCrory in turn held a 49.7 per cent interest in Glen Alden; and so, through a logical chain of command, Meshulam Riklis had a guiding hand in the actions of Glen Alden and *its* subsidiaries.

(Glen Alden, moreover, was soon to acquire the Philip Carey Company, manufacturers of building materials. Therefore this also would become part of the Riklis complex. Its sales would produce an additional $90,000,000 a year!)

In fact, all of 1964 and 1965 proved to be extraordinary. Not only did McCrory's earnings climb to over $9,000,000, as predicted by Sam Neaman, but the corporation was offered and quickly availed itself of another outstanding opportunity.

By early 1966 it had acquired approximately 70 per cent of the renowned S. Klein discount department stores — all ten of them. Neaman was named president of the entire retailing division.

In a report to stockholders Rik announced that sales "are now over $700,000,000 and should soon reach $1,000,000,000. Our program will place McCrory among the very top non-food retailing companies in the country. It will stand sixth in the nation — behind only Sears, Penney, Montgomery Ward, Woolworth, and Federated." Commenting on Glen Alden's contribution to the empire's total profits, Rik projected them to be an additional $13,000,000 to $15,000,000 by 1967.

Thus, scarcely more than a year and a half past the nadir of his career, he stood at the head of one of the country's major enterprises in retailing.

His activities had, of course, expanded to include other aspects of growth. For instance, as far back as 1961 he had helped to establish the McCrory Credit Corporation. This, in the words of its management, "functions as a centralized credit organization, servicing McCrory's operating divisions by purchasing accounts receivable and also advancing funds against receivables." The Credit Corporation makes it unnecessary to pay the costs of financing to outside agencies; its income becomes part of the cash flow of the Riklis empire.

Another subsidiary was called the McCrory Leasing Corporation. Its primary purpose was to operate the company's Distribution and Data Processing Center in York, Pennsylvania.

There were other subdivisions, too. An empire is not an uncomplicated thing. This one became more complex with every phase of its growth.

Still, Rik could see a possible weakness in the structure he had built. Could it ever be charged that Rapid-American was too small an entity to control so vast an empire? Would it not be wise to strengthen Rapid-American's own basic financial position in order to justify its leadership in this tremendous and expanding corporate complex?

For that matter, would it not be equally wise to add to his own holdings in Rapid-American? At this time he had only a little more than 5 per cent of its stock. The guiding spirit of a company ought to own more of its equity, he decided; and his unflagging confidence in the future of the organization made the purchase of such stock an irresistible urge. He began to buy all he could manage.

This would take care of his personal problem. But what about strengthening Rapid-American?

To accomplish this, he said to his board members, the Rapid-American Corporation ought to acquire *for itself* — not for McCrory, not for Glen Alden, but as part of its own identity — a large and prosperous company whose assets would be a source of strength and enrichment.

The board agreed. The search began.

Of all the suggestions which stockbrokers and private individuals sent to Riklis's desk, one stood out like a brilliant light. This was the men's clothing manufacturing concern known for more than half a century as Joseph H. Cohen and Sons. It was the largest in its industry. It grossed some $45,000,000 a year and showed profits of well over $4,000,000.

In several ways the needs and aspirations of its owners, Isidore Cohen and Wilfred P. Cohen, paralleled those of Albert List. Like List, they would have welcomed greater leisure in life, the opportunity to devote more time and energy to charitable and cultural pursuits.

Wilfred P. Cohen had an additional reason for seeking a diminution of business responsibility. He had become a remarkably successful painter, a career followed only in those hours he could salvage from his office. His paintings had enjoyed many exhibitions and sales in America and in Europe. Indeed, there was a time when, having known Willie Cohen for some thirty-five years and having watched the rise of his artistic success, I had written about his art in *Reader's Digest*.

Obviously the Cohen brothers were ready to listen to reasons for merging. The fact that Riklis was willing to pay $21,000,000 for their business was not to be ignored.

And so the Cohen Company became part of Rapid-American. It did not become a segment of McCrory, it should be noted; nor of Glen Alden; only of Rapid-American. The distinction is more than a matter of semantics. Increasing Rapid-American's own earnings by some $4,000,000 a year, this Cohen acquisition added to Rapid's stature, to its financial strength, to its dignity in the industrial world. Rapid-American at once assumed the proportions of an entity big enough to control its giant divisions.

"What pleased me as much as anything else about this deal," Rik said, "is that the same banks which had been worried about us in 1963 now happily lent us an extra $9,000,000 to consummate the Cohen purchase. It was an expression of confidence which I deeply treasured."

Prestige and strength were not the only benefits of the Cohen acquisition. As Rik has put it: "Taking advantage of this purchase, we were immediately able to sell $5,000,000 of preferred stock. Also using this, we merged into our Rapid organization another company that had cash and readily liquidated assets of *well over $8,000,000!*"

This was Hanover Equities, with real estate and banking interests.

A long time ago, in talking with Riklis, I observed that there is something almost Biblical in the story of his mergers. One always begat another, and this begat a third, and so it has continued. To what end? No one can say. Even the Bible never forecast any end to man's progress.

3

A naive young student once asked Rik, "Can you give me some idea of what a fellow can expect to earn in this merger business? I mean, after five or ten years?" It was a silly question, and Rik merely smiled. "If he's lucky and smart," he replied, "he'll earn enough to buy some more companies."

The truth is that Riklis was faring incredibly well only fourteen years after he got his first Minneapolis job. By 1965 his salaries as board chairman of McCrory's and of Rapid-American amounted to $221,688 a year. On November 24 — as reported in a new proxy statement — "provision was made to permit Mr. Riklis to receive in addition an annual salary of $50,000 as chairman of the board of the Glen Alden Corporation." Also, as a result of investing every dollar he could raise, he now owned 93,900 shares of McCrory common stock. The dividends his own shares paid, added to his salary, lifted his annual income to well over $300,000.

To put it another way, his income had doubled in almost every year since he had got his first job!

There was a day when I sat with Rik and his wife, chatting. I tried to induce her to give me her own appraisal of her husband's traits, business and otherwise, which had led to his present position. The conversation became a good-humored debate between husband and wife, a catalogue of amused disagreements. Yet it turned into a revealing dialogue.

"Rik likes to think of himself as a tough businessman," Judy said with a chuckle. "But when you really know him you realize that he is the same with businessmen as with his children — often soft and sentimental and, in a nice way, even emotional."

Rik looked at her in surprise. "Where on earth did you ever pick up such nonsense?" he demanded. "In business I'm cold, I'm calculating. Everybody knows that. I figure out what I want and I go after it."

"Unless you think it's going to hurt somebody."

"I don't *want* to hurt anybody," he conceded. "On the other hand, the only reason we've managed to get where we are is that I'm a bulldog. I hang on to what I go after — and *hope* nobody gets hurt."

She laughed with wifely mockery. Then she turned to me. "Were you ever around when somebody asked Rik for a loan?"

"No," I said. "Why?"

"He has a system all his own. You tell him you need a thousand dollars. Fine. If you're his friend he asks no questions. He gets out his checkbook and writes the check. Only after he gives you the money does he ask why you need it."

"By that time," he argued, "I figure I've *bought* the right to ask."

"It's given him the reputation of being an easy touch," Judy said.

"I'd rather be an easy touch than deny a friend the money he needs," Rik declared. "Especially if he's one of the Bleeders."

"Bleeders?" I repeated.

"That's what I call those who bled with me in 1963. The Bleeders. They supported me and they're entitled to ask anything they want of me. Always."

Judy laughed again. "See what I mean?" she said. "Real tough on the inside."

Soft or tough, by 1965 Meshulam Riklis had achieved a firm position in the financial world. He had repaid the personal debts he had incurred in 1963; and he had constantly used whatever funds he could raise to augment his holdings in McCrory's and Rapid-American. He was, one would have said, an extremely happy man — happy in his business, happy in the life he enjoyed with his wife and the children, Mona,

Marcia, and Ira. Now that the tensions of 1963 were a memory, he could indulge in the pleasures most of his associates enjoyed. He could play golf, tennis, own a boat, ski, collect art, travel.

Unfortunately, in the life he has led there has never been quite enough leisure for Rik to do *everything* he wants to do. Even now, when his secretaries try to discuss something, they frequently have to stride along with him as he hurries to keep an appointment for which he may be late. I have actually seen one of them take his dictation in a down-going elevator and read back to him as they crossed the building's lobby.

Not that this high-pressure existence always results in business success. There have been failures, too. A couple of years ago (to mention only one) Rik became excited by the prospect of acquiring the huge McKesson and Robbins corporation. He wanted it badly. It would have created a vast and profitable addition to his empire; it would have provided a new and widespread distribution system.

Through Glen Alden he offered to purchase McKesson and Robbins's stock. Over a million shares were actually bought. Rik was well on the way to acquiring control of the drug and food company when he suddenly learned that certain directors of McKesson and Robbins did not want him associated with their company. They were blunt in saying so to Rik's bankers. He was "a foreigner" and they wanted no part of him.

That was all Rik needed to hear. The offer for McKesson and Robbins's stock was limited and the shares already bought through Glen Alden were sold to Foremost Dairies, which also wanted McKesson and Robbins. Riklis "walked away" from the deal. Though it could have been one of his biggest, he dropped it without regrets, without comment, without any sense of defeat.

"Just one of those things that didn't work out," he said. As always, he refused to go where he was not wanted; refused to resort to a proxy fight. "There are better, more civilized ways of building an empire."

XIII

THE Federal Trade Commission has long had the right to challenge mergers if they are contrary to the public interest. Like the Antitrust Division of the Department of Justice, the FTC seeks to guarantee the right of competition.

The question generally is, *at what point* is power to be exerted? To what extent is it safe to permit merging to continue?

The dairy industry, for one, has been a source of many such problems. It has a history almost unbelievable in its reliance on mergers. As long ago as the 1940's it was disclosed that 75 per cent of Borden's growth was the result of mergers. Seventy-three per cent of Beatrice Foods' and 74 per cent of National Dairy's expansion were attributable to the same means.

The government did not intercede in any of these mergers as long as they involved small acquisitions. But when Beatrice Foods acquired five large firms with sales totaling $65,000,000, the Federal Trade Commission charged that these were illegal. For this was indeed reducing competition. The parent company was ordered to divest itself of its five new acquisitions.

Borden's, National, and others have similarly been forced to sell off divisions that made them so big as to lead to monopolistic dangers. There was, in the same category, the astonishing growth of Foremost Dairies, its sales rising from $58,000,000 in 1950 to $388,000,000 five years later. Challenged by the government, Foremost had to dispose of some of its equities.

Meshulam Riklis kept his empire out of such litigation largely by building it on lines which did not conflict with anti-trust laws. One could hardly argue that a combination of McCrory stores and RKO theaters, or of Lerner Shops and Philip Carey building materials constituted a threat to nationwide competition. The fact that the government has never challenged any of his mergers is a tribute to his selectivity and to his legal advisers.

Nevertheless the possibility of government interference always exists, and it brings up a curious problem: Is growth by merger more harmful to the economy than the growth of a company by internal expansion?

As a firm thrives by its own efforts, constantly becoming bigger and bigger and absorbing a greater share of its market, it is beyond reach of the law. The A & P stores, to pick an example, can open as many branches as they like, and no regulation will prevent such growth. But similar growth by merger can — and often is — checked because the government regards it as dangerous!

Former Assistant Attorney General Robert A. Bicks has said, "The basic assumption of the Clayton Act is that somehow growth by merger differs sufficiently in kind and in consequence from internal growth to warrant different treatment."

Bicks then suggested a hypothetical situation. "The case that would make a joke out of whatever difference may exist between the two sorts of growth," he said, "would be a case attacking General Motors' acquisition of a small calender company. The purchase by GM of a calender firm would have a real impact on the calender market. *But so would GM's expansion into calenders by internal growth, without acquisitions.* What would cause the impact? Probably no calender company has ever been managed by anybody as competent as GM or with the financial resources GM has, so you would have a competitive advantage that would stem solely from the very sort of factors that competition is supposed to promote."

Much as one may object to government interference with private enterprise, there are admittedly situations in which one must concede the wisdom of some agencies which are seeking new powers. The chairman of the Securities and Exchange Commission, Manuel F. Cohen, has for some time been asking greater authority over tender offers by corporations that pay *in cash* for the securities they buy.

The rationale for this is easy to understand. When a corporation offers to buy another company's stock through an exchange of securities, it is required to register its new stock issue with the Securities and Exchange Commission. In doing so it must disclose, in a formal statement, why it is making the offer. Thus the person being asked to sell his shares knows what a corporation proposes to do. He is in a position to determine for himself, on the basis of knowledge, whether he wishes to accept the offer for his securities.

Until now, however, a corporation offering to buy shares *for cash* has not had to be so explicit.

Chairman Cohen wants cash transactions to be subject to the same regulations as credit transactions. He argues with a good deal of logic that Corporation A, in offering to buy the stock of Corporation B, may have plans for activities that will send its stock soaring to high levels. Thus the man who sells his holdings to Corporation A may soon discover that he made a sad mistake. Had he retained his stock, it would have zoomed. The sale, in spite of any premium price he might have accepted, turned out to be a serious long-term loss. And his loss resulted from his ignorance of the corporation's plans. Chairman Cohen wishes to remove this hazard to the seller by supplying him with all the information needed for forming an intelligent judgment.

It is clear that in this and other matters the government will have to reappraise its position and clarify its thinking in respect to the benefits and perils of mergers.

2

They have had an international effect which is seldom discussed, perhaps because it is peripheral. Nevertheless it is worth taking into account.

In France, I once asked a manufacturer of perfumes why he did not establish an office in the United States, the principal consumer of his products. Why did he prefer to be represented in New York by an American firm?

The question elicited a sad smile. "I suppose I could earn a great deal more by the elimination of the middleman," he admitted. "But as I look at America and observe the huge combinations of various industries that are taking place, I draw back. Several other perfume manufacturers have already been drawn into mergers. Looking at them, I realize I have no way of knowing what my competition will be in the future. Will I be facing combinations which command billions in resources? I prefer to accept my present ratio of profits and to continue with my present methods. Why should I enter America and make an investment which may lead to such overpowering competition?"

I pointed out that there was a certain degree of protection in the anti-trust laws; but this merely brought a Gallic shrug. "When you can bring me assurances," he said, "that there will be no more giant mergers involving other perfume manufacturers, then we can talk about my coming to America."

At the same time a West German manufacturer of detergents and soaps also shook his head at the idea of competing in the United States. "In England," he said, "yes. I have a branch there. I also operate throughout the Common Market. But making a place for myself in the American market — where so many competing firms are becoming bigger and bigger through mergers — would require so much capital, so much effort, so tremendous an expenditure of resources and energy, that I prefer to stay out of it."

In a sense, then, one might say that America's mergers serve to discourage foreign competition.

3

Whenever anyone asks Meshulam Riklis if he considers the merger trend a good thing or bad, he replies that the answer lies in the *purpose* of a particular merger. It is good if its aim is to provide greater efficiency of operation, better service to the public, higher earnings for its shareholders, more liberal benefits for employees. It is bad if its sole motive is merely a greater concentration of power in power-greedy hands.

There are of course many ways of judging the merits of mergers; but one thing seems certain: they are inevitable in our time.

Can small producers meet the needs of a nation growing at an explosive rate? Could small producers give us the automobiles we require, the planes, the TV sets, the communication services which have welded together every corner of the world? Bigness can be a necessity, and a country's very security may depend upon the strength that emanates from it. To clarify the new atmosphere in which men like Riklis operate, we must recognize this change.

Only a few years ago all mergers were regarded as incipient trusts. Few people argued with Judge Learned Hand when he maintained, "Congress did not condone 'good trusts' and condemn 'bad' ones; it forbade all."

But today we have come to see that mergers do *not* have to result in trusts. Perhaps that was why the editors of *Fortune* magazine recently proposed: "Congress should amend the antitrust statutes to make it clear that . . . it is not the national policy to prefer any particular size, shape, or number of firms to any other size, shape, or number; and that mergers — horizontal, vertical, or conglomerate — are entirely legal unless they spring from a manifest attempt to restrain trade."

Sooner or later there must be a reevaluation of what we mean by "big" companies. We must reappraise their usefulness, weigh it on new scales against what may be called their dangers — if, in truth, there still are dangers in spite of all the laws and regulations we have evolved.

I have little doubt that more and more mergers must now mark the progress of American industry. Guided by the right people, they can do great service to the nation's economy.

4

As one might expect, the responsibility of heading a great industrial empire has brought about some marked changes in Riklis's methods of operation.

Only a few years ago the watchword at the Fifth Avenue offices was: *Rik makes all decisions.*

Things no longer happen quite that way. The members of the executive staff still walk into the chairman's office, without knocking and without much regard to what he may be doing at the moment. ("I like it that way," Rik says. "Informal. Makes us realize we're all pulling together.") But now the men come in more often to consult than to seek decisions.

For Rik has taught himself the wisdom of delegating responsibility. He has learned to say, "*You* take care of it. It's your problem."

He still makes major decisions. No doubt he always will. These involve matters of company policy. But the *implementation* of policy he leaves wholly to his associates.

"There was a time," he once confided to me, "when the unhappy experiences I'd had with deals like Gruen and Smith-Corona made me feel I must guide every move of our companies myself. I've come to see that this is no longer possible — or even intelligent. I now have around me an efficient and brilliant group of associates. These are all top-rank executives who have proved their abilities again and again. It would be ridiculous not to give their abilities full scope.

"So today my attitude is: once you give a man the responsibility for handling a certain situation, *let* him handle it. I'm available for any advice I may be able to give — if they want it. But when I see the fine work they do, when I see the rising line on the graph of our earnings, I know that the system of leaving a job to those responsible for it is the best way of serving our corporations."

If I have from time to time stressed Rik's philanthropic activities, it is because philanthropy has become a natural ingredient of American business success — a recognized obligation rather than a whim. Long ago, when I was talking with a Westerner who had given some $16,000,000 to various colleges, he said to me, "This country has been very kind to me. I started with nothing and wound up with everything. When I give away money it is because for me it is a way of saying, 'Thank you, America.'"

Does Rik share these sentimental ideas? Nobody knows. But I do know that once, when he was talking in a mood of confidential self-revelation, he confessed that what he was now able to do in philanthropy was one of the true rewards for all his efforts in empire-building.

"I should put the comforts I am able to give my family as the number one compensation I get for working," he said. "But definitely number two is the ability to give to these causes I've always wanted to support."

These are not causes chosen at random. High on his list are the people who have been left homeless by the political and ideological upheavals of the past decades. Jewish refugees from persecution have been his primary concern. He saw them by the hundreds of thousands in Israel. The swiftest channel for helping them has been through the United Jewish Appeal. To this Rik has given so generously that his home is filled with citations of appreciation.

(He has not concentrated *exclusively* on Jewish needs. Not long ago when Dr. Martin Luther King came to lunch at the McCrory offices, I learned in surprise that Rik had for a long time been contributing to Dr. King's struggles for underprivileged Negroes. He had been doing this years before Dr. King became a Nobel laureate.)

Second on Rik's roster of philanthropies is the need to

bolster religious institutions. Though he refuses to think of himself as an Orthodox, Conservative, or Reform Jew, but only as a Jew, he is as dedicated as his father to the fostering of Judaic culture, philosophy, faith. This, he feels, can best be done by training able men for the rabbinate, thus providing teachers for modern Jews. So he gives generously to institutions like the Jewish Theological Seminary.

He has been giving so generously, in truth, that in March of 1967 the seminary held a great dinner in his honor at the Waldorf-Astoria Hotel. Charles Bassine was toastmaster, and the principal address of the evening — a veritable paean of praise in Rik's honor — was delivered by New York's senior senator, Jacob K. Javits. The occasion celebrated a gift Rik had just made to the seminary — a huge communications building. And what will it communicate? "The beauty of the Jewish faith," Rik says simply.

Next in the line of need he regards those organizations which fight for human rights — and against the defamation of such rights. The Anti-Defamation League of the B'nai B'rith is a leader in this crusade. To it Rik contributes many thousands of dollars and many hours of service. In 1965 he worked so assiduously to win support for B'nai B'rith, and so successfully, that he was chosen its Man of the Year for his achievements. Here too he was honored at a dinner attended by some fifteen hundred of America's leading businessmen. And as he ate he was handed this letter:

My dear friend:

It has just been brought to my attention that you are about to be granted the 1965 Man of Achievement Award of the Anti-Defamation League of B'nai B'rith. For those who have selected you to receive this honor, it means that your life and achievements personify the fulfillment of the American promise.

You know the warm regard and pride with which I view your many accomplishments. You may live in New York, own properties around the country and travel around the world, but I know we have every right to call you a Minnesotan. We who remember your early beginnings and career as a Hebrew scholar and teacher, as a financial adviser and now a leader in the financial world, take great satisfaction in your accomplishments. We are proud that we had some small part in providing the encouragement that contributed to your outstanding career.

Your life and career are living testimony of the renewed strength and vitality that constantly reinvigorate the stream of American life as we admit into our society and into our honor roll of citizens people of dedication and principle without regard to creed, race, color or national origin.

I regret I cannot personally be with you and your many friends of the Anti-Defamation League as you receive this high award. You and they, however, have my warmest greetings and best wishes.

Sincerely,
Hubert H. Humphrey

Education has been another area of Rik's philanthropic attention. He recently endowed a chair at Brandeis University. And outside of Jewish circles, he persuaded his board of directors to join Albert List and himself in converting the former Lane Department Store (a tremendous building at Fifth Avenue and 14th Street in New York) to an annex for the New School of Social Research.

True, the major emphasis of his philanthropy remains Jewish. For Rik (this he will tell you with a great deal of pride once you have come to know him well) is the eighth-generation descendant of Baal Shem Tov, the renowned founder of Hassidism.

So hearing this man discuss financial transactions is in itself a paradox; eight generations of Hassidim probably expected their offspring to be a rabbi. Not a single one among them — except his father — could have understood such fantastic terms as bonds and debentures and warrants. I doubt if any of them had ever been constrained to deal in funds of more than a hundred dollars or so. Had any been told that their descendant, one Meshulam ben Pinhas, also known as Riklis, would one day be dealing in hundreds of millions of dollars, they would no doubt have thought they were hearing the rantings of a madman.

But they would have been pleased to know that his son Ira celebrated his Bar Mitzvah in Israel, returning to the same synagogue in which former Riklis boys had observed their own Bar Mitzvahs.

I have mentioned the catalogue of his philanthropies — and there are many more — not to applaud his generosity. Rather, I do it to emphasize the heavy and increased expectations society has of the businessman of our time. Accepted as a patron of everything from religion to education and art, he has supplanted the doges of sixteenth-century Italy, the kings of renaissance France, the rulers of Britain, even the Church of medieval times; and certainly the handful of people known as "The 400" of nineteenth-century America.

In the same way corporations are expected to play their part in meeting the country's cultural needs. This is, after all, the very core of the American credo — that private enterprise remain the supreme source of the nation's spiritual strength. And corporate financial help is evident in everything from universities down to Little League baseball teams.

McCrory has not been remiss. For example, like countless other companies that have assisted their employees and their children to further their education, McCrory's and its affiliates have favored their own. (Thus, as an example, McCrory's now awards to the children of its workers twenty four-year scholarships a year, each grant worth $4,000.)

During the summer of 1966 Riklis underwrote a unique study to discover the philanthropic needs his corporations could best meet. He engaged a noted clergyman — one steeped in social work — to spend his two-month vacation on a tour of the United States. He asked the minister to visit the principal cities in which there were McCrory stores and to ascertain the wisest way of using philanthropic funds in those communities. This provided guidelines such as few corporations have ever created for themselves. Perhaps it also provided a precedent.

Whenever anyone today asks, "What does it take to head a big corporation?" the answer must include this: it takes a profound sense of social responsibility; it takes an intelligent knowledge of where and how to distribute large sums of money; and it takes a willingness to give much of one's time and thoughts to philanthropic demands.

XIV

THERE are many lawsuits that rise out of misconceptions and fear on the part of stockholders: will a merger somehow depress the value of their securities? The bulk of these may be labeled as nuisance suits that are eventually dismissed by annoyed judges; actions that lack substance and logic.

Meshulam Riklis, like every entrepreneur in the merger field, has had his share of such suits. A typical one was brought against him and Albert List, jointly, by a lady who owned 125 shares of Glen Alden stock. When she heard that McCrory had bought more than 2,000,000 Glen Alden shares, not including hers, she rushed to her lawyer.

Why the attorney permitted her to bring this suit into court is a difficult thing to understand. Its allegations (there were over twenty of them) were founded on vague apprehensions, not on facts, and the damages she sought were nebulous. But even baseless charges, when bruited around Wall Street, can have the same effect as rumors. They can certainly serve to depress the price of stocks. Investors understandably hang back, waiting to see what will happen.

In this case the woman alleged that McCrory's purchase of 49.7 per cent of Glen Alden's stock was the result of "a secret deal" between Riklis and List.

The court found that there had been no secrecy of any kind. All stockholders of Glen Alden had been offered the chance to tender their securities to McCrory at the same price paid to Albert List. They had all received proxy statements. They tendered over 800,000 shares. The charge of secrecy was thus shown to be absurd.

The complaining woman further alleged that McCrory's was buying Glen Alden only to liquidate it. This could conceivably leave her 125 shares worthless.

Here her allegation was dismissed on two counts. First, there was no plan to liquidate Glen Alden; the sale of its coal and leather tanning divisions had been projected only to strengthen the company. As to the possible future worthlessness of the stock, the court took note of the fact that McCrory's itself owned 20,000 times as many shares as the complainant. The company would hardly be following the suicidal course of rendering its own holdings worthless.

Added to the woman's charges was one that Albert List was about to resign and leave the management of Glen Alden to strangers. In view of the fact that List had never resigned and that he had continued to be the chief executive of Glen Alden, this allegation too lost its point.

And so one charge after another was proved to be unfounded, and the judge dismissed the entire case. But it had taken the time and efforts of legal staffs. It had cost everybody concerned a great deal of money. Worst of all, it had stirred doubts among security analysts, stockbrokers, and others, and such doubts are hardly the best influences on a corporation's reputation. People remember the charges long after they forget the exoneration.

As one distinguished lawyer said, "Suits of this kind are

frequently brought against companies with the hope that the defendants will make a settlement payment rather than go to court and risk adverse publicity. Riklis happens to be the kind of man who won't pay what amounts to blackmail."

And he added, "Such lawsuits are the risk one must take in building an empire through mergers. The more active an entrepreneur becomes, the more legal actions he is likely to stir up. Fortunately the recent history of court decisions indicates that nuisance suits have little chance of succeeding. Perhaps this fact will discourage them in the future."

2

With Glen Alden, Joseph H. Cohen and Sons, and Hanover Equities added to the empire, Rik might have been expected to pause. There must be intervals during which one consolidates one's gains before proceeding to the next annexation.

Rik, however, did not pause very long. For some time he had been meeting with his friend Sol Kittay, head of the BVD Corporation. Talks about the possibilities of merging had been broached; and now, in 1966, they reached the stage of action.

The BVD Corporation itself, though originally a manufacturer of men's underwear, was a complex of several firms that Kittay had acquired over the years. Their directors had to be convinced — as did Rik's at Glen Alden — that a merger would hold advantages for them all.

One of the facts of life in corporate affairs is this: with every merger one or two new personalities are added to a board. These are generally men who have made their own successful careers — men of strong wills, of intelligence, of perspicacity.

In such a grouping of individualists one might expect to find sharp disagreements, outright conflict. So it is extraordinary to realize that a merger with so large an entity as BVD roused no opposition of significance among the directors of either corporation. There were a number of differing opinions, of course, on the best financial procedures to be adopted. But such matters, often deferring to the advice of Financial Vice-President Isidore Becker, were quietly resolved.

I emphasize this for a purpose. It indicates the importance of creating *human* synergism in corporate ventures. It is not enough to have a smooth meshing of firms. It is equally urgent to have a smooth meshing of personalities. And this Meshulam Riklis has managed to achieve, perhaps intuitively, by making close friends of many who work with him.

The BVD negotiations continued month after month, committees meeting several times a week, with Leonard Lane and Isidore Becker representing McCrory at many of these sessions.

Curiously, no one talked any more about Rik's inexperience as a retailer. He had disarmed his former critics, if any still remained, by defining his own functions as compared to those of others. "I regard myself as the *financial* head of our organization," he said. "I regard others as the *management* people. Sam Neaman runs the McCrory-McLellan-Green stores, the Klein stores, and the entire soft-goods division except, of course, Lerner's. Harold Lane continues to run the Lerner Shops. Down in Tulsa the Sanditens operate Otasco's four hundred outlets. As for Glen Alden, that's in the hands of its own management. And the Cohen brothers are responsible for men's clothing. Let me add another name here to the fine kind of management we now have — I mean Leonard Lane's because of the way he has taken on and rehabilitated the RKO theaters. We have management that is efficient. Everybody knows it. It is one of the strongest advantages we have to offer anyone with whom we may merge in the future."

Rik's comment on Samuel Neaman was founded on many remarkable developments. It had been Neaman's destiny to take hold of various enterprises at times when they needed a fresh managerial approach. This had been true of the McCrory stores in 1963. It had been true of the Klein Department Stores. Under Neaman's management every retail division of the empire quickly soared to profitable times; so quickly that one banker said to me, "Of all the investments Riklis has made I'd say Sam Neaman was one of the best."

Neaman's basic skill, it has often been said, lies in being able to divide even the most complex problem into its simplest component parts. He has, as one of his colleagues expressed it, "a keen, swift, and discerning eye for what is functioning poorly; and, just as important, a practical sense of how to make it function well."

No modern retailer has achieved so extraordinary and widespread a record for turning disappointing earnings or even losses (as in the case of the Klein stores) into thriving, profitable ventures. If the McCrory Corporation is now noted for its efficiency, Rik has said, much of the credit must go to Neaman. "He personifies management of the highest order."

The RKO theatres too, under Leonard C. Lane's supervision, have become a gratifyingly profitable division of Glen Alden, and Leonard Lane's presence on the board of McCrory's has become synonymous with able management.

Financially the merger with BVD proved invaluable to the empire. For one thing, it raised total sales by $131,000,000 a year. For another, it increased assets to a level never before attained.

How did it affect Rik himself?

Seventeen years earlier, when he was contemplating acquisitions like Marion Power Shovel and Balcrank, any deal that involved more than a million dollars seemed enormous. His friends whistled at the thought. Some shook their heads and decided he was reaching too far.

Now in 1966 and 1967 he could no longer consider any deal as *small* as a million dollars. It would make no sense in his empire. With the cash and assets at his disposal (there were total current assets of almost $150,000,000) Meshulam Riklis was finding it futile to discuss any merger that involved less than $25,000,000. He was, indeed, aiming at some far greater.

Several corporations which, like Rapid-American, have been seeking mergers during the past few years have published booklets intended to guide brokers. These pamphlets describe precisely the kind and size of acquisitions a firm desires. Mallory and Company has one of the most detailed. Others may be less precise but they nevertheless make their needs clear.

"Such information saves everybody a lot of time," Jerome Hollender of Shearson, Hammill told me. "Nobody goes to Mallory with the wrong kind of suggestions. What's more, the booklets make us understand that these firms are not expanding in a helter-skelter way. They each have a plan, a program, a target. They know where they're going and how they expect to get there. That's a good thing in the field of mergers. It shows they're becoming scientifically selective, well planned, well thought out."

Rapid-American has not issued such a booklet. "We don't have to do it," Rik said. "Brokers we've talked with know by this time that we're interested only in certain types of acquisitions." He has made it clear that any project suggested to Rapid-American, McCrory, or Glen Alden must meet one or more basic requirements. It must tend to:

a. Add to financial strength and earnings.

b. Provide strong management.

c. Yield capital for additional growth.

d. Create a broader market for products and services.

e. Diversify operations.

f. Offer a way of utilizing tax losses.

g. Open new avenues of distribution.

h. Assure control of a projected acquisition.

i. Add to the prestige of the empire.

Unless a broker can make a strong case for one or several of these stipulations, Riklis is not interested.

The Best department store chain was an offer that clearly met his criteria. This acquisition was accomplished with surprising speed; it took only a few weeks to consummate. At the time it occurred there were rumors that it would become part of the S. Klein discount complex. But Rik and Sam Neaman quickly corrected this impression.

"We have no intention," Rik said, "of making this a discount operation. Best's on Fifth Avenue in New York and in many suburbs has a fashion reputation. We want to retain that. Its present management will continue to operate as in the past, but under Sam Neaman's general supervision. The Best stores will add diversification and a touch of luxury appeal, if you wish to call it that, to our entire retailing picture. We can say of them what we must be able to say of every acquisition: they fit into our pattern."

Is there such a thing in business as "transference of ability"? Will a man who is able in one position be equally able in another? Or will his efficiency fade as he is moved to responsibilities for which he has had no training?

Leonard C. Lane's success with RKO theaters, Sam Neaman's skill in operating retail establishments — careers like theirs suggest that good businessmen can be effective wherever they may be placed. One wishes this could always be true; but the sad fact is that many a saltwater fish perishes when tossed into a freshwater lake, and many a freshwater fish dies in the ocean.

Meshulam Riklis's problem in finding able management to run his acquisitions was usually solved by the retention of former management if it was functioning well. This is the system most merger entrepreneurs have found most satisfactory.

"If you are building a conglomerate empire," Rik has said, "you cannot hope to be an expert in every field you enter. You *have* to rely on experts to work for you. In all likelihood these men got their training within the acquisitions you make. So the formation of conglomerate mergers does not *reduce* the number of executive posts available to good men. At the head of every division there are just as many jobs as there always were and there is just as much opportunity to get ahead."

The records of almost every organization founded on a

conglomerate pattern confirm Riklis's assurance that management jobs are seldom sacrificed. A complex like Litton Industries, one of the most spectacular of all merger empires, proves the point. Almost one hundred different firms now constitute Litton's holdings. They deal in such variegated areas as cash registers and space exploration, shipyards and display cases. The number of products they sell exceeds nine thousand. Both Board Chairman Charles B. Thornton and President Roy Ash agree that their own function is to "manage management." Wherever possible, they retain and help the management they acquire. And this is done with an incredibly small headquarters force, less than two hundred in Litton's case.

Textron, with twenty-eight companies marketing products as dissimilar as helicopters and fountain pens, follows the same policy of "letting management alone as long as it is efficient." Its chairman, Rupert Thompson, once told an interviewer, "Buying an outfit that has to be restaffed is anathema to Textron."

Walter Kidde, Gulf and Western, I. T. & T., Ogden — indeed, virtually all the major operators in the merger field try to follow this course. Norton Simon of Hunt's Foods is perhaps an exception. He seems to specialize in buying companies that are having rough times *because* of poor management. He frequently makes a point of changing that management as quickly as he obtains control of a firm. Since Simon does not hesitate to buy into a corporation that needs improvement, his procedures are understandable — and amply vindicated when new management turns a loss operation into one that is profitable.

Let me make it clear that I am referring here to management policies in *conglomerate* mergers. What I have said about retaining management does not necessarily apply to *horizontal* mergers.

Where similar firms dealing in similar products are wedded to one another, it is often good business, economy, and the very secret of profitability to create one central management which eliminates many separate managerial forces.

A vivid example is the Consolidated Oil and Gas Company of Denver, Colorado. Its chief executive officer, Harry True-blood, was once an oil engineer. Working for a number of small oil companies in the Southwest, he noted that practically all of them were either losing money or showing scant earnings. Not that they lacked oil; all were producing and selling it. They were simply not converting it to profits, and True-blood could see why.

He did what Meshulam Riklis had once done: he formed an investment syndicate among friends in his home town, Denver. Backed by their funds, he began to merge small oil companies. Within a few years he had formed a complex of fourteen.

The fourteen divisions of his organization sold no more oil than they had in the past. *Yet now they showed a remarkably good profit ratio.* At the time I discussed this with Harry Trueblood I based a magazine article on his experiences and called it "Loss Plus Loss Equals Profit." What Trueblood explained was this:

"It was uneconomical to have fourteen different sets of management doing practically the same thing. So we created *one* management staff. Instead of having fourteen presidents drawing an average of $50,000 to $75,000 each, we had one president — with a $35,000 salary at the beginning. Instead of having fourteen sets of vice-presidents and other officers, we had only two vice-presidents. We paid rent and office over-head on a single headquarters building here in Denver — thereby saving the cost of rent and overhead in thirteen other cities. We saved more money by installing a single billing operation. In fact, we saved money on every aspect of management you can mention by eliminating thirteen offices and their staffs. Thus, on the same income we had before the mergers were effected, we turned fourteen losses into a very satisfactory profit."

The Trueblood example is impressive for its delineation of one way horizontal mergers can help borderline firms — those not yielding the full returns of which they are capable. As Meshulam Riklis once learned about variety stores that did not pay, and as Leonard Lane learned about theaters that did not pay, the sooner you closed them the better off the company became. The same is true of management that does not pay: the sooner it is eliminated, the sooner investors may see their stock begin to rise in value.

One may sympathize with those who lose executive jobs because of horizontal mergers. But as Harry Trueblood remarked, "These mergers would not have taken place if there hadn't been unprofitable management to begin with. So let's not blame the theory of mergers. Let's blame a situation which was uneconomic, inefficient, and without profit before the mergers took place. We were the physicians, you might say, who had to take firm measures. No surgeon operates just for the sake of operating. He operates to cure."

XV

"CAN a little fish swallow a big fish?"

This is one of Riklis's favorite queries. He uses it when analyzing the possibility of acquiring a firm much bigger than his own. Can a company merge with one larger than itself, yet come through the merger as the surviving corporation, its name and status intact?

Obviously the answer is yes. The very existence of Rapid-American testifies to this.

In 1966 I had talks with Rik in which he mentioned his next goal — "a little fish going after a big one." This would be the acquisition of the largest of all the corporations he had ever considered. *The deal might demand the investment of some $300,000,000!* If it was consummated it would lift Rik's empire to the $2,000,000,000 mark, perhaps even beyond it. Assuredly it was a prize worth patience and effort.

To finance such a transaction would require the assumption of debt beyond anything the empire had attempted in the past. "No matter how you undertake a $300,000,000 obligation," Rik said, "you're going to have to pay interest on it. At 6 per cent you will be paying $18,000,000 a year."

We were talking over lunch in his office. He paused to let the interest figure make its impression.

"But surely," I argued, "you would be paying a good part of the $300,000,000 in cash. That would reduce the remaining debt on which you'd be paying interest."

"We would want to *have* the cash with which to pay," Rik corrected. "That would assure banks and investors that we *can* pay. But we would still prefer borrowing rather than using our capital. Therefore we would have to be in a position to pay the $18,000,000 interest before we could undertake a merger of this size."

"Are you in that position?"

"We've been building up to it for several years."

That puzzled me. "You mean you've been aiming at this $300,000,000 deal since 1963 or 1964?"

"That's right."

"Even while you were going through the McCrory ordeal?"

Rik shrugged. "You've *got* to dream a long time ahead," he said. "And you've got to dream on bad days as well as on good days. We've always been preparing for steps like this one."

Suddenly many aspects of the past year fell into clearer focus. In 1963 Rik's objective in generating cash had been to rescue McCrory. But even with that necessity past he had continued to pile up cash assets. And he had succeeded by steps which, in retrospect, became meaningful in a new way.

The acquisition of Joseph H. Cohen and Sons had served to strengthen Rapid-American's earnings position; the clothing company was pouring some $4,500,000 in earnings into Rapid-American's treasury.

Also — and now I grasped its reason as I never had before — the empire had recently sold to the public 49 per cent of Lerner's stock. This had raised enormous amounts in cash. Yet it had left McCrory's with a 51 per cent controlling interest in Lerner's.

And there were more things to remember. The merger with the BVD Corporation, whose sales were over $130,000,000 a year — indeed, all these steps which had been taken in the past year or two were aimed not at aggrandizement for the sake of becoming bigger. All were aimed not only at strengthening McCrory's and Rapid's position but were part of the grand plan for purchasing the $300,000,000 behemoth.

As I watched Rik across the luncheon table I felt certain that even this newest $300,000,000 acquisition, when and if it occurred, would also be only the forerunner of larger ones. You can no more check the growth of an enterprise like Rik's than you can check the growth of a child to an adult. Such an empire cannot long stand still. It can either shrink by liquidating its holdings; or it can grow through internal expansion and continued acquisition; or both.

There is no longer anything extraordinary about a small fish like Rapid-American swallowing a bigger one. Joseph Rosenberg of the Empire Trust Company presented a long list of such transactions in *Barron's* magazine. By way of demonstrating the fact that financial writers often think in the same metaphorical terms, he called his article "Minnow and Whale."

He wrote, for example, of how the Williams Brothers Company, with a net worth of $23,000,000, acquired the much larger Great Lakes Pipe Line Company for $287,600,000. The Williams Brothers Company managed this by using only $9,600,000 of its own money. They arranged to raise the remaining amount by obtaining $150,000,000 from institutional investors in exchange for debentures. Great Lakes stockholders themselves would take $60,000,000. The rest would come from bank loans and the issuance of new convertible securities.

"After it's all over," Mr. Rosenberg wrote, "Williams will wind up with a company with earnings almost ten times that generated by its own pipeline construction activities. The prospect of smallish Williams Brothers successfully pulling off such a coup predictably has sent its stock soaring. Back in October, before the news was out, the shares traded at no higher than 20. Last week they traded at 89."

If this can be regarded as a typical case, it is obvious that it can pay very well indeed for a small company to acquire a bigger one. When the PUB United Corporation borrowed $26,000,000 to acquire the famed Rheingold Breweries, the price per share of its common stock rose, in a two-year period, from 6½ to 27.

There is, too, the record of the Rollins Broadcasting Corporation, with annual sales of only $8,000,000, buying the giant Orkin Exterminating Company, the largest pest-control organization in the country, with annual sales of $37,000,000. Again this was accomplished by borrowing almost all of the $62,400,-000 involved in the purchase. And how did the deal benefit "little" Rollins? Its shares rose from slightly less than 5 to over 51!

All these, manifestly, are illustrations of what happened when small companies bought bigger ones in order to add to their earnings. But there are many such acquisitions made for what may be called *indirect* earnings: like the purchase of a large corporation that has been showing a loss in order to use the loss as tax carry-over. A recent classic case occurred when the Storer Broadcasting Corporation borrowed $34,000,000 to acquire a major interest in the debt-ridden Northeast Airlines.

Northeast, after several difficult years, had suffered losses of $50,000,000. By law the Storer corporation could apply these to offset its own earnings as long as it continued to operate Northeast Airlines. Use of the tax-loss served to increase the value of every Storer share by $12!

Will the time come when Northeast will prove a drain on Storer? Indications are that this is hardly likely. By throwing new energy into the management of Northeast, its current earnings have been increased. And the rising incidence of air travel promises well for the future. Storer has arranged for the purchase of twenty-two jet planes which it will *lease* to its subsidiary, thus creating an additional way to supplement its own earnings. It now appears that this small fish will have little trouble in digesting its very big meal.

Considering all such transactions (there are countless more) it becomes evident that Riklis was not aiming too high in planning for his $300,000,000 acquisition.

"I think," he said, "it can be the best thing that ever happened for our stockholders, for our employees, and for everybody else concerned."

Would the corporation be able to provide sufficient collateral to borrow the huge sums involved? To make certain such collateral would be on hand, it decided to buy back a million shares from its stockholders — *if they would sell.*

2

When, as an observer, I attended a meeting of McCrory's board of directors in February of 1967 it was almost inconceivable that only three or four years earlier many of these same men had confronted the company's possible collapse. Gathered around the long conference table — at which there were representatives of three banks — they were all cheerful and optimistic.

There is nothing like success to stimulate cordial feelings at a board meeting. When Chairman Riklis announced Mc-Crory's estimated earnings for 1966 — an announcement which would become official with the annual report to stockholders — I looked around the table at a collection of contented smiles. The earnings were exceeding every figure that had been hoped for a year ago. The Lerner division alone was showing after-tax profits of over $6,500,000! The S. Klein division had in a single year been rescued from losses and placed in the earning columns. All was going well. Combined 1966 earnings for the companies in which Rapid-American had an interest would surpass $32,000,000!

Haim Bernstein told me, "It may be snowing outside, but this is one of the sunniest days I've seen in here this whole winter."

But success has its penalties. When a company sets out to buy its own shares back from the public — as the Riklis empire was offering to do — it sometimes happens that investors become shrewdly suspicious. Would Rapid-American or Mc-Crory be buying its own securities unless it had reason to know that their value would soon increase? And if that were so, why sell? Why not hold on and wait for the rise?

This is not the only reasoning which may deter shareholders from immediately responding to a tender offer. As the New York *Times* explained in analyzing the reluctance of investors to part with their stock even at a premium price:

> In deciding whether to accept the tender offer, the stockholder has to take into account such things as income

tax considerations, the chance of another offer at a higher price and the possibility that he will not receive the tender price for all the shares he submits.

Another consideration is that the announcement of a tender offer frequently focuses attention on a company whose record has been largely ignored by investors.

This attention may result in a competing tender offer or a merger bid from another company, in which case the stockholder has to figure out which situation might be the most profitable.

Still another possibility is that the tender-maker might make a new offer at a higher price if it does not receive all the shares it was seeking at a lower price.

Last December, for example, Fifth Avenue Coach Lines made an offer to buy 260,000 shares of Austin, Nichols & Co., a liquor distributor, at $20 a share. The stock was selling for around $14 a share at the time and Fifth Avenue received about 100,000 shares.

Unable to get all the shares it wanted, Fifth Avenue made a second offer in March, this time at $27.50 a share when the market price was $22 a share.

Shareholders who accepted the first offer received $6 a share more than the previous market price but missed out on the additional $7.50 a share in the second offer.

Commenting on the situation, Victor Muscat, chairman of Fifth Avenue Coach, declared: "This is a brand new deal. The market price now is only as high as it is because of the first tender offer, and that offer is over."

Riklis and his directors were well aware of the public's probable attitude when they offered to buy their stock. Finan-

cial Vice-President Isidore Becker reported that he had regis-
tered with the SEC the corporation's offer for a million shares
if tendered within a certain period, and his announcement
brought skeptical headshakings at the board meeting.

Director Leonard Spangenburg said, "My guess is we'll be
lucky to get 600,000 shares."

Vice-Chairman Lane, slightly more optimistic, put the figure
at 700,000. Of the fifteen men around the table not one
believed the full million shares would be tendered. Director
Seymour Lazar skeptically asked a colleague across the table,
"Would *you* sell under the circumstances?" After the comment
Rik informally spoke about his hope of realizing an acquisition
in the $300,000,000 class.

Oddly, no director had any apprehensions about Rapid-
American or McCrory becoming *too* big by taking this step —
that is, so big as to incur government disapproval. After the
meeting I spoke with most of the men. Not one foresaw any
difficulty. "This acquisition has no connection with our soft-
goods retailing division," one director assured me. "It will not
represent undue concentration of any industry under a single
ownership. The government has no reason to object."

Another man waved the subject aside by saying, "Bigness in
itself is neither unethical nor illegal. We have nothing to worry
about."

Still, on the same day that this board meeting was held,
Newsweek in its business columns was reporting the uneasiness of International Business Machines because of *its* bigness.

IBM had managed to capture 68.3 per cent of the entire
computer business in the United States — not by merging but
largely through its own skill and internal expansion. It was so
far ahead of competition that the next in line, Honeywell, had

only 7 per cent of the national market. All the rest of the companies were smaller.

"For nearly a decade," *Newsweek* reported, "International Business Machines has dominated the huge and growing computer industry with all the awesome efficiency of one of its own mechanical brains — and for nearly that long the industry has wondered when this dominance would catch the Justice Department's trust-busting eye. Last week, after a flood of rumors of an investigation, IBM itself decided to ask antitrust chief Donald Turner if they were true. Turner's answer: yes.

"IBM has always taken care to avoid mergers that might bring antitrust attention," *Newsweek* added. "Still, its marketing practices trigger envious fury in its competition. Rivals complain that IBM's gambit of announcing new machines months or years before marketing them leads customers to postpone buying competitive models that have beaten IBM to the punch. No one could guess what might come of the investigation, but the sensitive antennas of Wall Street quivered. IBM's stock (which had reached a new 1966–1967 high of 404½ that week) *fell off 11½ points on the news.*"

If the IBM situation can be regarded as an omen, even self-made bigness — in other words, success without mergers — can threaten government activity, which is strong enough to depress a company's securities.

But *can* government in the long run really check legitimate growth? Once, when I put this query to Meshulam Riklis, he said, "Nobody can stop the growth of American business any more than he can stop the growth of a tree — unless he chops it down. As long as government and industry cooperate as they should, helping each other every step of the way, you will see business grow in wealth. That means the country, too, will grow in wealth. Mergers are merely an expression of today's swift *need* of growth. I think they are the most exciting and healthiest thing that has happened to the American economy in our generation."

"Are you planning any mergers in Europe?" I asked.

That seemed to startle him. "Why do you ask?"

"Because it's a trend. Over two thousand American companies have made mergers in the Common Market."

"Manufacturers," he pointed out. "Not retailers."

"That's true, but — "

"Look," he interrupted with a smile. "Whether or not we'll ever expand in Europe, I can't say now. There's still plenty of growing we can do in *this* country. When we come to the end of our American possibilities — well, ask me that question again!" Then he added more seriously, "Mergers have been one of the great stimulating causes of the European recovery. Europe's debt to them is tremendous."

3

Not that everybody agrees with Rik on the value of mergers. In various conversations I have had with Robert M. Bleiberg of the Dow-Jones Corporation — an eminent economist, editor, and writer — Mr. Bleiberg has expressed the opinion that "full returns on the future of the merger age are not yet in by any means." Most mergers, Mr. Bleiberg maintains, are possible only in an era of easy credit. They *depend* on credit.

"At the moment," Bleiberg said, "credit is still fairly easy to obtain — in spite of the government's 1966 scare when the Federal Reserve suddenly tightened credit lines. That scare was a harbinger. It showed what *could* happen. There is another factor to keep in mind, too. During years of steady inflation such as we have been living in, banks realize that the dollars they lend today may be paid back ten or twenty years hence in dollars worth far less. This should make bankers hesitant in assenting to too many long-term sizable loans.

"Once you change the easy credit period to one of tight credit, corporations are going to find it exceedingly hard, if not impossible, to finance as many mergers as we see today. I'm not at all sure that a small fish, as you call it, *will* always be able to borrow enough to swallow a big fish. We may soon be approaching the end of a twenty-year era of easy credit. And if the end comes, if borrowing to finance mergers is restricted, you will certainly see a great change in modern business methods."

"Do you think, then," I asked, "that men like Meshulam Riklis and others involved in mergers will not be able to function as they do today?"

"I don't see how they will be able to operate without the credit support they now have," Mr. Bleiberg said. "They couldn't have built their empires thirty or forty years ago — that is to say, starting with nothing as Riklis did. And I doubt if it will be possible thirty or forty years in the future. We may be witnessing a phenomenon peculiar to the middle decades of this century. But, as I say, it is a bit early to talk with complete assurance. We will have to watch closely to see what the next few years bring."

I must express my own belief that easy credit — and therefore the age of mergers — will be part of our economic life for many decades to come. There are reasons few economists like to mention. At the risk of sounding cynical I must say that if there is such a thing as leverage in borrowing — using debt to increase debt — there is also such a thing as leverage in *lending*.

I can readily see the predicament of bankers who can save an investment in a huge, floundering company only by lending it more money to reestablish a solvent position. If a company owes $100,000,000, let us say, the banking community simply cannot accept a $100,000,000 loss without trying to rescue itself. It *has* to help the borrower regain a profit-making position so that he may pay his debts. And if this procedure involves the escalation of credit, so be it. There is little alternative if a loss is to be avoided.

The era of mergers, then, is likely to be with us for a long, long time since corporations have to increase their size and earnings not only to compete with one another but to meet mounting financial obligations.

One need not be an economist to realize that in times of easy credit great loans are made, and the more a bank lends the more capital it needs. So we witness an era in which banking institutions (which, after all, *make* their money by *lending* money) are all but pleading with the public to borrow more!

Never before — as has been pointed out to critics of easy credit — has the personal loan business of commercial banks been so brisk. This is largely because banks constantly *advertise* the credit policies of their personal loan divisions. Lately, in conjunction with credit-card organizations, they have offered to make borrowing so easy and automatic (up to $5,000 per person) that one signs no papers at all. One enjoys a personal revolving credit which one can use at will, simply by writing a check for amounts larger than one's bank deposit. The charge is generally 1 per cent per month on the amount borrowed — or 12 per cent a year at simple interest. This in turn brings the bank that much more in earnings, that much more to lend to others.

Is this a vicious circle of indebtedness? I am not at all sure whether history will call it "vicious," "clever," "wise," "liberal," "frustrating," or "brilliant."

It will not be the lack of credit which will eventually put a brake on merger operations. If it is anything at all, it will be the government — and only in the case of those mergers which begin to absorb so many components of their industries that competition and fair trade will indeed threaten to turn into a struggle among a few giants. That, obviously, is a situation which must be avoided. But in the future it will be avoided by laws and regulations, I suspect, rather than by the denial of credit.

XVI

IN MANY ways Meshulam Riklis reached in 1967 the pinnacle of his career thus far. All was going well. His empire officially announced total 1966 earnings of more than $32,000,000.

"With that amount flowing in," I suggested, "you can afford to sit back and consolidate your position."

"With that amount flowing in," he replied, "I've got to plan on how to put the money to the best possible use." He waved toward documents on his desk. "All these are merger or acquisition possibilities," he said. "Not that we're in a hurry. From this point on we're going to be more selective and more deliberate than ever. But we have no intention of sitting back and doing nothing. We will *develop* what we have and at the same time we will add new equities as we feel they will benefit our stockholders, our employees, and everyone else."

"What about the $300,000,000 deal? Think it will come to a head soon?"

"If we're lucky, very soon."

I have several times referred to the contemplated $300,000,-000 acquisition. It promised to be a dramatic climax, a clash of cymbals, as it were, in an exciting orchestration. If I did not identify the company it was because it could not be named while negotiations were in progress. But by March of 1967 there was no further need for secrecy. The company at issue was the great Schenley Corporation.

For more than a year and a half Rik had been attempting to reach an agreement with Schenley's head, Lewis Rosenstiel. Sporadic conversations had been inconclusive, yet Rik had always been optimistic. "Rosenstiel isn't the kind of man you can hurry," he said. "I'm willing to be patient. It took many years to build Schenley's. It's worth waiting a year or two to acquire it."

The plan to buy Schenley became an office obsession. Everybody from vice-presidents to secretaries knew about it, whispered about it, rolled their eyes toward the ceiling and said, "May it happen soon!" The board of directors voted Rik full powers to proceed in whatever ways were necessary.

With the enormous combined assets and borrowing power of Glen Alden at his disposal he foresaw no problem in financing the Schenley purchase. As for his directors, all manifested confidence and pride. Added to the other Riklis enterprises, Schenley would make the empire one of the largest corporate entities in the nation.

In early March Rik flew to a conference on the West Coast. During his absence, while discussing Schenley with Haim Bernstein, I tried to put into words a curious uneasiness I felt.

"It seems to me," I said, "that Rik has his heart set on Schenley more strongly than he's ever felt about any other acquisition."

"Naturally," Bernstein agreed. "It's the biggest deal of them all."

"What if it doesn't go through?"

Bernstein looked thoughtfully at a window. "I suppose he'll be heartbroken," he finally said. "But he won't show it. Not Rik. He'll grin and say, 'So we'll go for another company. You can't buy them all.'"

"He's been building up to this one as if nothing else really matters."

"Don't you believe it," Bernstein said. "Remember I once told you he's like a good chess player. He always has an alternate move in mind in case the original one doesn't work."

Curiously, apart from a vague apprehension, I had no reason to suspect anything would go wrong with the Schenley plans. And then all the financial columns suddenly reported that Lewis Rosenstiel of the Schenley Corporation had decided to merge with the *P. Lorillard Tobacco Company!*

I did not see Rik that day. He was still on the West Coast. But I did see the reaction of his stunned office force. They appeared to regard what had happened as incredible. How could Mr. Rosenstiel have negotiated with Lorillard or anyone else while the Riklis project was pending?

I asked one of his secretaries — he now had three — if Rik had telephoned. "Not yet," she said. She added in a whisper, "He'll feel terrible!"

Two days later Rik was back at his desk. Coming in to see him, I had the uncomfortable feeling that condolences might be appropriate. I expected to find him angry and disappointed.

Instead he smiled with the same warmth he always showed as we shook hands. When I tried to tell him how sorry I felt about the collapse of the Schenley dream, he said, "So we'll go for another company. You can't buy them all."

It was several days later, toward the middle of March, that

Rik was being driven from his King's Point home to a meeting at the Waldorf-Astoria Hotel. He had dropped his two younger children, Marcia and Ira, at their school as he did every morning, and now he settled back to read a newspaper while the chauffeur sped toward New York.

He turned to the stock market quotations. After checking several prices he glanced at the Schenley listing. It was at slightly more than 58¼ — a price to which it had leaped since the possibility of the Lorillard merger had been announced.

There is always a telephone in Rik's car. Shortly after nine he called his office. His secretary said, "Mr. Becker's been wanting to talk to you. He says it's urgent. I'll switch you over."

Financial Vice-President Isidore Becker sounded tense. "Rik, there's a rumor that the Schenley-Lorillard deal *fell through!*"

Rik said flatly, "I don't believe it. Has anybody checked?"

"Everybody's checked. But nobody at Schenley's or Lorillard wants to talk."

"Where's Mr. Rosenstiel?"

"Somewhere off the coast of Florida on his boat. Can't be reached."

Rik hung up the telephone and settled back to think. He considered the situation all the way to the Waldorf-Astoria.

At 9:30 he was scheduled to deliver an informal talk on mergers and acquisitions to a group of company executives. Somehow he got through the extemporaneous speech quite well; it was quoted extensively in the *Wall Street Journal*.

But throughout the address no listener could suspect that half his mind was fixed on the Schenley rumor; and somewhere during this discourse on mergers Rik reached a decision.

As soon as he had answered the last question from the audience he hurried to a telephone booth. He called investment banker Bernard Cantor in Los Angeles.

"Bernie," he said, "I want you to put in a bid for 200,000 shares of Schenley at 50. Immediately. For our Glen Alden account."

"Schenley closed at 58."

"I know it. I still say 50."

It would take $10,000,000 to buy the 200,000 shares at 50. Glen Alden's strong cash reserves were at last being put to use.

Cantor said, "At 50 it could be a hell of a good buy — if it goes that low."

"If it doesn't, I'm not buying and I'm not losing anything," Rik said. "On the other hand, if we do get the 200,000 shares and the Lorillard deal is off, we'll have a good piece of Schenley when we resume negotiations. And if the rumor *isn't* true, Schenley will go up again, and we'll make money. Buy the 200,000 shares."

What neither Rik nor Cantor knew was that a Swiss syndicate — never identified — had just offered 250,000 shares of Schenley to be sold. Perhaps the rumor of the merger's failure had alarmed them; they wanted to take their profit while it could still be had.

At any rate, with so much uncertainty about the Schenley-Lorillard future, the stock exchange suspended trading in the securities for a single day. When business resumed the next morning, the price was down, and Rik got his 200,000 shares at $50 a share!

That same afternoon both Lewis Rosenstiel and Lorillard officers were reached by the press, by stockbrokers, by investors. Both sides indignantly denied the rumor of a collapse of negotiations. Both assured all questioners that the merger was indeed scheduled to go through; there was not even a hint of its failure.

Instantly the price of Schenley stock skyrocketed. Within twenty-four hours it went up 11 points to $61.

Meshulam Riklis was back on the telephone. "*Sell* our 200,000 shares," he ordered.

The following day every New York newspaper and hundreds more throughout the country carried the story of the deal that had earned $2,200,000 in a single day. The *World-Journal-Tribune's* report began:

> Meshulam Riklis, 43-year-old head of a billion dollar empire, pulled off one of the biggest coups in the recent history of the stock market by reaping a $2 million net profit this week on the sale of 200,000 shares of Schenley Industries.

That happened to be a day when I had been asked to lunch with Rik, Isidore Becker, Robert Miller, and lawyer Harry Wachtel. They were in buoyant spirits. All morning telephone inquiries had been coming from newspapers and news magazines and financial writers. Rik's picture was in every paper. He himself was in an almost benign mood. At some point over lunch I again asked, "Rik, what's going to be next now that you've lost Schenley?"

Before he could reply Robert Miller interposed, "Let's not talk about Schenley as a *loss*. We just made $2,000,000 out of Schenley! We could use that kind of loss every day of the year!"

I glanced at Rik. He was smiling as he nibbled at his lunch. If he had been hurt by the collapse of his Schenley dream there was still no outward sign of disappointment. I remembered the philosophic words Bernstein had predicted and which Rik had repeated: "So we'll go for another company. You can't buy them all."

2

Within a week Meshulam Riklis was again in the newspapers. This time it was because, as the *Wall Street Journal* began its report, "McCrory Corporation sales and earnings for the fiscal year ended January 31 reached new records. . . ."

Indeed, every division of McCrory was doing remarkably well. So it was in an atmosphere of confidence and high spirits that Rik talked this particular afternoon, again drawing circles on a yellow paper.

This time we sat at his desk. The first circle was at the top of the sheet. It represented the Rapid-American Corporation. Rik's faith in its future was so strong that he was buying as much of its stock as he could. Only a year ago he had owned just over 90,000 shares. Now he owned more than 400,000, including preferred stock and warrants. He hoped before long to have 600,000, which would give him a personal equity of approximately 20 per cent in the company.

He drew a spur jutting from the circle to a small square he labeled "Joseph H. Cohen and Sons." This top segment of the organizational chart, he explained, represented the parent company, Rapid.

"Now here is McCrory-McLellan-Green," he said, drawing a

larger circle beneath the first. "McCrory embodies our whole retailing enterprise. To it we have added Lerner's, Otasco, the Klein department stores, the Best stores — in fact, this circle contains the entire retailing division. Like Rapid-American it will be permanent and unchanged except for the normal growth we have projected for it. This includes new variety stores and at least five new Klein stores. With Sam Neaman in charge of the operation, it is increasing its earnings in ways no one dreamed possible a few years ago."

Now he drew a line below McCrory's, connecting it to a third large circle which he marked "Glen Alden." Spurs jutting from this symbolized the Philip Carey Company and BVD.

"This," he said, "is the area to which we are going to bring our new acquisitions. Glen Alden will grow as a great conglomerate. I have high hopes for it."

I considered the billion-dollar diagram he had drawn, knowing there were many segments he had not included, like the RKO theaters, the several companies which had come into the complex with BVD, a few other Glen Alden subsidiaries.

"Rik," I said, "I have never known you to be without a plan in mind. Your wife claims that even when you're home your thoughts are on companies and opportunities all over the country. Where do you go from here?"

He nodded as if he had been expecting the question. "My first objective," he said, "is to increase the earnings per share of Glen Alden. It is now earning about $1.40. I want to increase that to $2. I expect to do it with the next acquisition, whatever it may be."

"How?"

A generation ago a businessman would have replied, "We'll

produce more, sell more." Now Rik's answer was a revelation of the way the modern entrepreneur thinks and works.

"I'm looking for a company that shows earnings of $5,000,-000," he said. "If we can add five million to Glen Alden's earnings, it will increase the earnings of every Glen Alden share to the point I'm aiming at — $2. To get a company earning $5,000,000 I may have to pay ten times earnings, or $50,000,000. I'm ready for that. In fact, with our cash and borrowing capacity in Glen Alden, we can buy a $150,000,000 company. *That's* the kind of deal I'm really looking for. I can no longer be interested in small deals. They would mean nothing to our setup."

Not many years ago only a prankster would have talked in terms of buying a $150,000,000 entity. Now in Rik's office discussions of such transactions are quite normal.

"What puzzles a good many people," I suggested, "is the fact that a company earning five or ten million should consider letting itself be merged into another company. I can understand the reasons a smaller firm might have. But a hundred-million-dollar corporation — "

"If it's open to merger discussion," Rik interrupted, "there's usually one main reason: *it could earn more!* Its stockholders don't think management is doing everything it could or should do. Earnings of $5,000,000 may not express the full potentials of a company. Stockholders would welcome better, more profitable conditions."

Rik rose from his desk, pushed his hands into his pockets, and began to pace the office. As I watched him I could not help noting again, for the thousandth time, the fine things with which he had surrounded himself here as in his home. There were striking paintings, many of them by distinguished Israeli artists; there were remarkable pieces of sculpture. In fact, through the open door that led to a lounge I could see a huge, headless, wildly exotic nude sculptured by Rodin. And dominating all other works of art was a life-size portrait in oils of Judy Riklis.

"Merging is the fastest and safest way of growing today," Rik said. "Fast, because you can *immediately* increase your earnings; safe, because you are buying a company that has already proved itself."

Rik's career has made one thing apparent: America is in the process of producing a new kind of financial leader. No longer will we identify an outstanding businessman by a single achievement — Vanderbilt and his railroads, Rockefeller and his oil, Astor and real estate, Ford and automobiles, Hearst and newspapers, Schwab and steel, and so on. In their place we now have a group of men whose wealth emanates from the wide diversity of enterprises they merge into empires. Merchant princes have bowed to emperors of finance.

Will there be a limit to their growth?

"We already have certain limits set by the antitrust laws," Rik says. "If more barricades are raised against growth, it will be in some degree the fault of those entrepreneurs who want to become so big that they *dominate* industry. That cannot be permitted. It will be bad for the nation. Mergers are simply another expression of free enterprise. We've got to make them with good sense, with sound purposes and judgment, and not out of avarice and vanity."

One does not need to be a soothsayer to predict that the increase of mergers will stimulate even greater activity on the part of government agencies. At this moment nobody seems to know which segment of the American population needs the most protection: the investing public, the corporations, the banks, or small business. Assistant Attorney General Donald Turner of the Antitrust Division has repeatedly assured questioners that his department is studying new methods of procedure. One of his assistants told me somewhat ruefully, "We ought to have a Riklis in our department."

If one were to sum up the Riklis career to this point — even if one were to start from the lowest depths of 1963 from which he had to fight his way back — one would come to a simple conclusion. Meshulam Riklis has disclosed a view of what the future promises. And he has proved that the United States is still what it has always been, a land of bright opportunity for those with imagination and energy. The fact that he came from another part of the world is in itself inspiring and reassuring, for it indicates that the doors of America are as open to foreign-born ability today as they were generations ago.

As far as his influence on industry in the United States may be appraised, Rik has been an economic catalyst. He has made things happen. He has brought ferment to some areas where stagnation threatened. If he has been a genius with numbers — as so many have said — it is appropriate to recall that philosopher Georgio de Santillana once remarked: "Numbers, according to Pythagoras, take a man by the hand and conduct him unerringly along the path of reason."

Rik's contributions to the American economy were dramatically recognized in May of 1967. President Johnson asked him to represent the United States on America Day at the international industrial exposition in Budapest. It was, in a sense, a way of presenting him to the world as a worthy example of the opportunities inherent in the American system. It was also a most remarkable compliment to one who had been a citizen for less than fifteen years.

Of course, I would hardly call him a typical American businessman, neither in what he has accomplished nor in his temperament; *especially* in his temperament. For one thing, he is too calm. It has become a fetish among certain industrialists to think of themselves as makers of quick decisions. "When something tough has to be done I don't hesitate to do it," they say. "I act." When you analyze the statement it can suggest that the executive may be acting foolishly. He is saying in effect that he never takes time to think, to weigh, to meditate on his actions. He rushes ahead by instinct.

Long observation makes it clear that Rik has never been in this category. When he makes what are apparently quick decisions, they are usually the product of long thought and planning at times when nobody is around to disturb him. "I wish," his wife said to me, "that his associates could see how he spends long hours every evening and over weekends. He sits there staring into space and studying papers. He might as well be a thousand miles away, paying no attention to anyone or anything around him. This is what precedes the things they call his quick decisions."

Rik himself says, "Long-range planning is my primary job, and you can't plan without thinking — or learning what others think. At the office I sometimes provoke my associates by asking blunt questions. They may sound like challenges; they may even irritate. But I do it deliberately in order to learn what my colleagues have in mind."

The system works well. By the time Rik makes his decision he has absorbed the thoughts of all the men around him. It has helped him, in a short period of sixteen years, to build one of America's most exciting industrial structures. With this as a foundation, where will the next sixteen years carry him?

No one ventures to guess.

By Way
of Epilogue

A BOOK should have a purpose, and it is fair to ask the purpose of this one.

Is it only to tell the story of Meshulam Riklis? No. That could be done within the confines of a magazine article. Is it only to discuss the increasing prevalence of mergers? No. That is evident to anyone who reads the financial pages of *The New York Times* or who subscribes to *The Wall Street Journal*.

Why, then, *did* I write this book?

I wrote it because I have dynamic confidence in the opportunities America still offers to people with imagination and energy. I wrote it because I have little patience with those who say the "good old days" are gone; that in the current state of our society no one can ever again become a millionaire; that no one can hope to compete with established Big Business.

A career like that of Meshulam Riklis vividly demonstrates that all such negative observations are untrue. It is just as feasible to amass millions today as it has always been. Only the methods have changed. In fact, we now have more millionaires than ever before. This can indeed be called a golden age for acquiring fortunes.

What we should ask is: What do men *do* today with their money? Do they make it benefit others as well as themselves?

And what qualifications, if they can be categorized, are now necessary to win financial eminence?

The lives of men like Riklis provide many interesting answers. When we analyze the ingredients of Rik's rise, for instance, we find that almost the first requirement for modern business success must be a creative, farsighted imagination. One must not fear, as *The Man from La Mancha* put it, to dream impossible dreams, to reach for unreachable stars. Was it absurd for Rik to envision a multimillion-dollar empire, with himself at its head, when he was earning $100 a week as a Hebrew teacher and a junior security analyst? Certainly it seemed so. Yet he showed that a dream is as strong as the determination behind it.

If men like Rik prove anything at all, it is that, with a dream formulated, one has to be a self-starter. "Nobody is going to drive us toward wealth; this is a course we ourselves must take," Rik has said, and it means simply that one must be able to generate the inner energy, the motivation and enthusiasm, the *action* that lead to success. At the risk of being berated for sermonizing, I must add that I have never met a self-made individual who did not share Rik's ability to drive himself toward a goal. Inertia is mankind's constant enemy. It has cheated countless people of the success they might have enjoyed if only they had overcome lethargy.

Again basing a judgment on Rik's career, no asset seems more important than persistence. He has never allowed himself to be defeated or even stopped by setbacks. "I have been accused of being like a racehorse with blinders," he once told me. "All I see or care about, they said, is the track ahead. Well, that might be a fine quality if I really had it. But the truth is I do get diverted."

I see nothing to regret in being diverted from one's goal — that is, temporarily — if the diversion itself is worthwhile. I saw Rik "get diverted," if that is the proper phrase, during the Israel crisis in June of 1967.

From the moment Nasser massed troops on Israel's borders and blockaded the Gulf of Aqaba, Rik plunged into the job of bringing assistance to the democracy that had for so long been his homeland. He headed a United Jewish Appeal Emergency Drive for funds among merchandisers. He poured his own money into the campaign and helped raise many millions more.

And I saw Rik "get diverted" again when he helped organize a committee whose purpose was to rouse all Americans to strive for security and peace in the Near East. This was not a Jewish committee; its membership was drawn from all faiths. Its aim was to protect *American* rights in the Near East — rights which might be completely lost if the Soviet Union's influence were permitted unchallenged sway among the Arab nations.

For it was not only disaster to Judaism that Rik foresaw if Israel were destroyed. Israel, an outpost of democracy, was a symbol of freedom. If it were annihilated (and some Arabs were still demanding this in the councils of the United Nations) freedom and democracy throughout the world would be dealt lethal blows. Rik flung himself into the struggle to avoid the holocaust. "Ask not for whom the bell tolls," he said to those he recruited for his committee. "It tolls for thee." And because he was right he was joined by scores of outstanding citizens representing industry, the professions, the arts.

These manifold activities, however, never interfered with the hours he devoted to business — which is why I say that in his case, as in the cases of many others, a primary requisite for financial success seems to be a dogged, single-minded dedication to one's job. Diversions come, yes; they are part of a man's social responsibility; but they cannot be allowed to interfere with corporate responsibilities. The business hours, Rik has frequently said, belong to the stockholders.

But stockholders, too, have come to appreciate the community duties of corporations and their officers. They understand the public relations benefits of having companies participate in community affairs. I have attended stockholder meetings at which men actually rose to ask why there was not a *greater* show of corporate interest in public affairs.

It is a curious thing, however, that after one has listed a few of the characteristics required for success in business — or in life, for that matter — one invariably faces those qualifications which only moralists used to mention: integrity, for instance.

A leading banker once said to me, "A reputation for integrity, for keeping one's word, is the basic qualification for any man who hopes to deal in big transactions. He will always need financial backing and he will get it only if people know they can trust his word. A man like Riklis may have many talents which he uses in the interests of the corporations he heads. But not one of them is as important as the fact that we all know he keeps his word. If he tells me over the phone that I will have a million dollars on Monday, I need no promissory note to that effect. I know the money will be on hand as promised. He has made that clear time after time. And though I don't want to sound like an echo of Horatio Alger, I cannot help making this point about the fundamental need of integrity if one is to climb to a position of success and stay there."

234

And one must return to the other sources of a man's abilities — his spiritual background and the contributions to his character of those who surround him.

As for Rik's spiritual background, it lies in a heritage that provided him with profound devotion to an explicit moral code. No man could ask a clearer guide to ethical conduct than the teachings of Torah and Talmud, and in these Judaic concepts he has been well trained. Indeed, he continues to seek training. He prizes his close association with many Jewish scholars; and I have noticed that at least half of the books he reads deal with problems of religion and metaphysics.

And as for the influence of those closest to him, I have tried to indicate the strength he has always drawn from his wife. Judy's undeviating confidence in his future, her constant encouragement of his aims, have in great measure been the bedrock on which he has built. If ever he hesitated to risk the future on an idea, she has been able to tell him with her quiet humor, "What are you worried about? If things go wrong we can always give Hebrew lessons."

He has been fortunate, too, in the training he received from parents who possess all those characteristics Rik himself reflects. Pinhas Riklis, his father, has a calm, intelligent, profoundly philosophical view of life. It was this inheritance, I suspect, that helped sustain Rik, with optimism and faith, through every trial of his career. From his mother he has gained not only more of this same spiritual quality, but also an inexhaustible fund of energy, determination, quick perception.

Though all these influences have gone into the making of the man, perhaps the most engaging thing about Meshulam Riklis is his refusal to pose as a self-satisfied, successful industrialist who has arrived at a destination. He is still on the way. He is as eager to take the next step in his career as he was years ago; more selective, it is true, and less hasty, but no less ambitious.

In fact, his inability to remain inactive has resulted in additional growth even since I wrote the last chapter of this book. He added to his empire by concluding a merger with the Stanley Warner Corporation. Stanley Warner is the parent company of such divisions as International Latex — in itself a tremendous enterprise — and of the 114 Warner Brothers theaters. Its addition to "the Glen Alden circle" of Riklis's diagram lifted that area of the empire toward its own billion-dollar-a-year sales.

And then, to the amazement of many Wall Street brokers, the Schenley Corporation and the P. Lorillard Company abruptly broke off their merger negotiations. The principals involved simply could not agree on terms.

Immediately after this announcement was made Rik was once more in touch with Schenley's head, Lewis Rosenstiel. Will the old dream become a reality? "At this point nobody can know," said one broker. "But if *anybody* can swing this deal, it's Rik."

On a recent occasion I asked Rik in a jesting way what he thought I ought to call this book. It is a study of mergers and acquisitions, of course, but also it is the record of his odyssey through the mazes of American finance. Here he was, the head of gigantic corporate interests at the age of forty-three, a magician who had forged an empire out of nothing except an idea and the courage to enact it. What book title did he consider appropriate?

He thought a moment, then grinned and said, "Why don't you call it *This Is the Beginning?*"